CW01655050

PLACES AND FACES ALONG THE CLEVELAND WAY

Photographs by Simon Calgie
Text by Debbie Chetham

HUTTON PRESS
1992

Published by the Hutton Press Ltd.
130 Canada Drive, Cherry Burton, Beverley
East Yorkshire, HU17 7SB

Printed and bound by

Clifford Ward & Co. (Bridlington) Ltd.,
55 West Street, Bridlington, East Yorkshire,
YO15 3DZ

ISBN 1 872167 37 3

CONTENTS

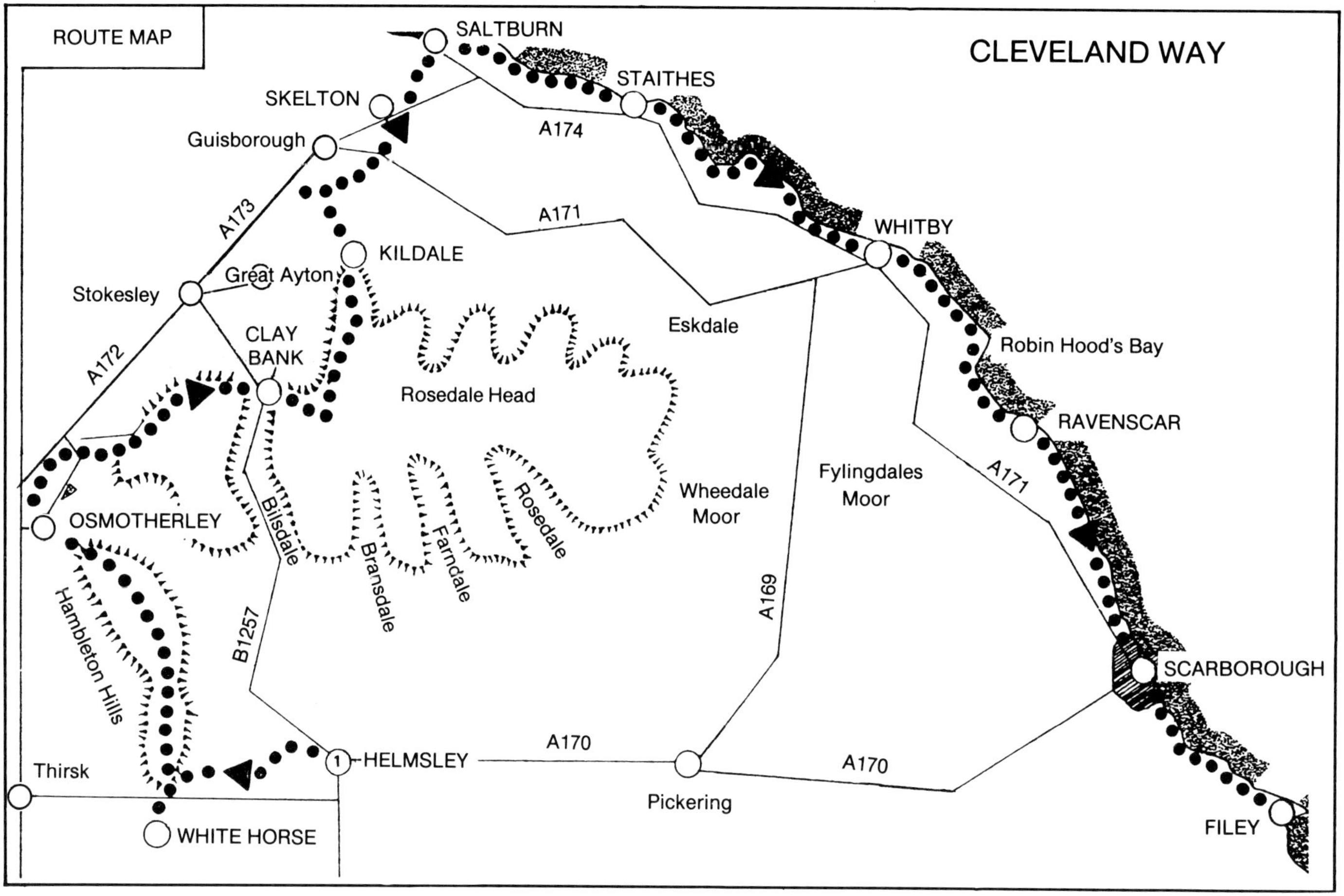
ROUTE MAP
CLEVELAND WAY
SALTBURN
SKELTON
STAITHES
Guisborough
A174
A173
A171
KILDALE
WHITBY
Great Ayton
Stokesley
Eskdale
CLAY BANK
Robin Hood's Bay
A172
Rosedale Head
RAVENSCAR
Fylingdales Moor
Wheedale Moor
A171
OSMOTHERLEY
Bilsdale
Rosedale
Farndale
Bransdale
Hambleton Hills
A169
B1257
SCARBOROUGH
A170
Thirsk
1
HELMSLEY
A170
Pickering
WHITE HORSE
FILEY

INTRODUCTION

THE Cleveland Way — a 108-mile walk? I'll never manage that in a thousand years. Simon's suggestion ... my reaction.

But I did! It's an achievement that gave me a great deal of pride, left those who know me reeling with shock and resulted in a series of features for the *North East Evening Gazette* — the Cleveland newspaper on which we both worked.

From those articles was born the idea for this book. Not a guide book giving inch by inch directions (there are plenty of those about), not a text book detailing the area's history and geography (I'll leave that to local academics). Rather, we wanted to produce a book which, through its photographs and accompanying text, would appeal to walkers and armchair athletes alike; to natives and to visitors. All need have only one thing in common — a love of the countryside through which the Cleveland Way runs.

Whether you are seeking solitude or somewhere to take the family; a stroll or a stiff hike; sea air or a sense of England past, there is a spot on the Cleveland Way to suit your needs. Little wonder therefore that the path is, in its third decade of existence, attracting thousands of new fans each year — far more than its founder, office-worker Alec Falconer, could ever have envisaged.

As one of the first members of Middlesbrough Rambling Club, it was way back in the 1930s that Alec first took groups up on to the Hambleton Hills, along the Cleveland escarpment and down the East coast cliffs. Today, there's more than one memorial to him on the route in appreciation of his pioneering ventures, but, at the time, the National Parks Commission (now the Countryside Commission) was in no hurry to approve his idea of a long distance footpath. It finally did so in 1952.

Then, it was referred to as the Moors and Coast Path. Its present title, suggested by Alec's son Alan, was not adopted until some years later. It originates from a route used centuries ago by traders on the moors and East coast who exported wool and imported wine at the port of Hull. The path they took was known as the Cleveland Road or Way. Never could the traders have imagined that they would, in the distant future, inspire many thousands of folk to follow in their footsteps — and this time just for fun!

Alan Falconer died in November 1991 but only a few months earlier he had shared with us his memories of how first his father and then he had become hooked on walking.

He remembered how, before the First World War, his father would disappear for a couple of days' lone hiking as a way of avoiding family gatherings which he hated. Later, when home for the holidays from Oxford University, Alan would join his dad on these weekend walks, often beginning in the Osmotherley area and going along the ridge of hills before turning east and heading for the coast. But it wasn't all in the name of fitness and fresh air.

"When I first started walking I was, like my father, on the look out for some good cream cakes," admitted the retired teacher of history and games. "And during the war, we were after vegetables that were normally on ration. We would go out and come back with our bags loaded with potatoes, pears and apples, and sometimes a bottle of cream and some farm butter."

In the last few years of his life Alan was rarely able to walk more than two miles at a time, although he tried to do that three times a week in woods local to his home near Middlesbrough. And while he was concerned about the erosion of the Cleveland Way through so much usage, he was also delighted that so many people were enjoying the countryside that had given the Falconer family so much pleasure over the years.

"Oh yes! I like to see people walking," said the man who proudly boasted that he had never worn a pair of walking boots in his life! Fittingly, Alan passed away, aged 82, while resting in his favourite armchair after one of his regular strolls. "It's how he would have wanted it," said his widow Ella.

The Cleveland Way as we know it was eventually launched in 1969. Unfortunately, the creation of and negotiations over public access had taken so long that its innovator, Mr. Falconer senior, was not around to join in the celebrations. He had died the previous year, aged 84. The route eventually decided upon fell almost 100 per cent within the old North Riding. However, local government reorganisation in 1974 put it over two counties — North Yorkshire and Cleveland — as it winds its way from Helmsley to Filey.

If you study a map of the region, you'll see the Cleveland Way forms a shape reminiscent of the two sloping sides of a triangle. The imaginary base line has since been named the Missing Link and it is possible to walk right back to your starting point. There are even plans in the pipeline to eventually upgrade this section to National Trail status but that's another story. The traditional Cleveland Way gives you plenty to be going on with — magnificent views and attractions, both natural and otherwise, to which you will want to return again and again, in all seasons. And don't let its overall length deter you from sampling its delights.

A survey carried out in 1989 by the National Park's first-ever Cleveland Way project officer, Ian Keirle, revealed that only just over a third of people using the route are actually out to walk the whole lot. The majority undertake journeys of less than a day's duration, of which the Cleveland Way doesn't necessarily play a total part. So use this book to choose a section that appeals to you and is within your walking capability. That way, there's no pressure to be at a certain place by a specific time. Just go as you please, stepping on and off the path wherever is convenient.

Alternatively, a similar tactic can be adopted to help you complete the whole distance. By getting together with another car owner you can, as we did, divide the route into sections and have transport to and from either end. This practice also alleviates worries about missing the last bus home or not having a suitable coin to 'phone for a lift when your feet refuse to go another inch. In this way, you are at the other side of Scarborough before you know it (well, almost!).

Should you be dependent on public transport, a free booklet called Moors Connections is an essential companion. Because it's designed with the walker in mind, this is not just a timetable of all bus and train services in the North York Moors, Ryedale and Malton region, but a guide to the best stops for alighting on and off along the Cleveland Way. Available from Tourist Information Offices, National Park centres and bus companies, the pamphlet is updated twice a year to keep it as accurate as possible.

All the same, there's nothing quite like a challenge and the fitter country-lover will not be able to resist completing the Cleveland Way in one fell swoop. This can be done in about eight days, stopping off in youth hostels, guest houses or camping overnight. An accommodation list, now including prices and facilities, is available from the North York Moors National Park, The Old Vicarage, Bondgate, Helmsley, North Yorkshire, YO6 5BP.

It's from there that the strategy document and work programme initiated by project officer Ian Keirle, before he moved on to pastures new, will continue to be studied and implemented where necessary by his successor to ensure that the Cleveland Way can be enjoyed by all its users well into the next century. This will involve maintaining and, in the well-trodden areas such as the path over the Cleveland Hills that also forms part of the Lyke Wake Walk and the Coast to Coast walk, improving and protecting. One way of doing this is to keep the casual walker off such sections by publicising the attractions of other parts. The main objective, according to Ian, will be to look at the Cleveland Way as the backbone of a whole network of paths and circular walks.

"We are happy, in the long term, to encourage more long distance walking and get more people to the coast but, at the moment, not onto the hills," Ian explained to us before leaving the National Park for his native Wales. "Initially, three years were set aside in which to implement the plans, but I see the work as never-ending."

Footpath repairs certainly will be, but the National Park may not have such a difficult task with its user policy if surveys and questionnaires already completed are anything to go by. They reveal that the path already plays a much wider role than as a gentler alternative for hikers to the Pennine Way and that it benefits not only ramblers too, but the economy of local communities along the route.

In return, these communities give the Cleveland Way its unique identity, unrivalled by other long-distance treks. Residents in the villages and towns en-route are proud of their heritage and of their modern-day environment, be it one influenced by farming, fishing or even the mining industry. If you take time to stop and chat, your experience of the Cleveland Way will be much the richer for it.

Alan Falconer – he wrote the very first guide book to the Cleveland Way, the route his father devised.

Long walks from little acorns grow – the symbol of the Cleveland Way.

Still standing – the East tower of Helmsley Castle.

Cleveland Way project officer, Ian Keirle, sets us on our way.

Chapter One

HELMSLEY

IT WAS a cold, damp, foggy, January morning when we arrived in Helmsley to explore the picturesque town that serves as the launch pad for the Cleveland Way.

From here, many months earlier, we had set off with blister-free feet, loaded rucksacks and not a care in the world, save that of eventually reaching Filey safely. As for many thousands of walkers before us, the delights of the North Yorkshire market town had gone almost unnoticed, so keen had we been to make our mark on the 108-mile route.

Then, the sun had been beating down, the streets teeming with tourists and the tea-rooms — of which there are a fair few — full to the brim. Today could not be more different. Certainly there will have been busier days for the town's market traders. There's been a market in Helmsley since at least 1467, although it was originally held in the churchyard. These days, the gaily-coloured canopies of the stalls brighten up the main square each Friday. At any other time, the area is dominated by the central statue of Baron William Feversham who died in the last century and whose descendants still own much of the surrounding land.

Whatever the weather though or time of year, a friendly atmosphere pervades and it is for this reason if none other that a delayed start on the Cleveland Way is to be urged in favour of a leisurely stroll not only around the town centre but the castle ruins and nearby Duncombe Park estate.

There is more to the castle than meets the eye. To the uninitiated, it appears to be in ruins but closer inspection reveals that this Norman fortress is not just a heap of ancient rubble.

Set behind the tall East tower that can be seen from the northern approach roads into Helmsley, is the less obtrusive West tower and the adjoining hall, combined to create a mansion for the lord and his family in the 16th century. Still in good shape, the main hall has been renovated and decorated in Elizabethan style. Another room houses exhibitions. Outside, visitors can wander over the beautifully-lawned grounds and bridged moat.

The site, now a favourite haunt of sleepy pigeons, was home to the local bigwig for nigh on 600 years until it was abandoned in 1711 for a residence on the adjacent Duncombe Park. That was when the Bedfordshire-based Duncombe family decided to take advantage of the estate they'd bought back in 1689 in order to establish themselves as North Yorkshire land magnates. So successful were they — in building houses, creating gardens and parks, representing the area in Parliament and marrying well — that, in 1826, Charles Duncombe was created Baron Feversham and, less than 50 years later, his grandson William given an earldom.

Their achievements though are totally overshadowed by those of the present Lord Feversham. When he inherited the house through an indirect line, it was being used as a girls' private school. But as soon as there was a gap in the lease, Lord Feversham ignored all advice to turn it into a money-making hotel or golf club and, instead, fulfilled his childhood dream of bringing the estate back into the family.

In 1985, he and his wife embarked on a ten-year plan to restore the house to its original and glorious state. Although it was badly-burned in the late 19th century, floor plans and inventories were saved, enabling restoration, then and now, to remain true.

The present decor, fabrics, furniture and colour scheme are all the Fevershams' own choice based on information gathered from history books, experts and trips around other period houses. It's hard to imagine that walls now lined in luxurious silk were once covered with shelves of schoolbooks and that six beds once made up a dormitory now almost filled by one enormous four-poster. The work is nowhere near finished, but

Early morning mist in Helmsley's All Saints churchyard.

when, bang on schedule, it was opened to the public at Easter 1990, it attracted more than 20,000 visitors that first season.

The lived-in look is not a clever marketing strategy but evidence that, unlike National Trust properties, this is still a family home and, even though the Fevershams have separate living quarters, they do use many of the restored rooms when Duncombe House is closed to the public between October and Easter. According to administrator Helen Cameron, only the best is good enough for Duncombe — there is no skimping, even in the parts the public will never reach. The cost remains firmly under wraps but when you consider the roof repair bill was £½ million and specially-made curtains are £10,000 a throw, it's not a project for the faint-hearted or penniless purse! Says Helen: "Some people think Lord Feversham is mad; others admire him for what he is doing. He is very much the local squire, very much involved in the local community."

Impressive though the house is, it is the park itself that attracts most attention. Its 35-acre garden has been described as a "supreme masterpiece of the art of the landscape gardener", but the land extends much further and vast expanses of it can be admired from the Cleveland Way as the River Rye comes into view.

Future plans for Duncombe Park include restoring the deer park and creating a couple of short walks within the grounds. One will take the visitor along the river, the other a 2½-mile route at the back of the estate. Both are designed to encourage appreciation of the countryside on foot. Says Helen Cameron: "We feel there is an audience whom we can introduce to the countryside with shorter walks and help by showing the way so they don't have to get out the map and work out routes. But then they might take the experience further and go longer, independent walks."

Talking of which ... that's what this book is supposed to be about! It's difficult not to get way-laid in Helmsley. Even just making your way to the market cross — the starting point for the Cleveland Way — there are so many distractions.

Breakfast on the banks of the River Rye.

There's All Saints church for example whose steeple dominates the skyline and where is kept a letter from the explorer Dr. Livingstone to Mrs. Gray, mother of the parish's best-known vicar, the Rev. Charles Gray, in charge for 43 years until 1913. Protected from the destructive qualities of light by a small piece of elaborate cloth, you have to search carefully for the letter, but it's worth the detour to learn of the doctor's gratitude for his gift of a mosquito curtain — the "handsomest" ever seen in the country, he writes.

Another place worth a glance or two if you have the time is Phoenix Forge down Boro Gate where there's been a forge for more than 200 years. The present blacksmith sells more wrought-iron flower baskets than anything else — there's at least one example outside every building in the street! — but they are still made using traditional skills and it's fascinating to watch him at work. Spectators are welcome all year round.

It would be wise though for you health-conscious hikers to resist until after your walk the temptation to sample the local brews served in the welcoming ale houses (four of which can be found in Market Square alone) or to enjoy the tasty traditional fayre found on the menus of a variety of cafés and restaurants. Despite the frequency of such eating places, and gift shops, Helmsley has thankfully not become a rural equivalent of Blackpool prom, but remains a provider of vital services to surrounding villages and farming communities. However, its country air cannot compare with that to be found on the surrounding hills and dales as experienced on the Cleveland Way. And so, at last, we go!

Chapter Two

First Section:

HELMSLEY
TO
SUTTON BANK
10.2 miles
TO
OSMOTHERLEY
11.4 miles

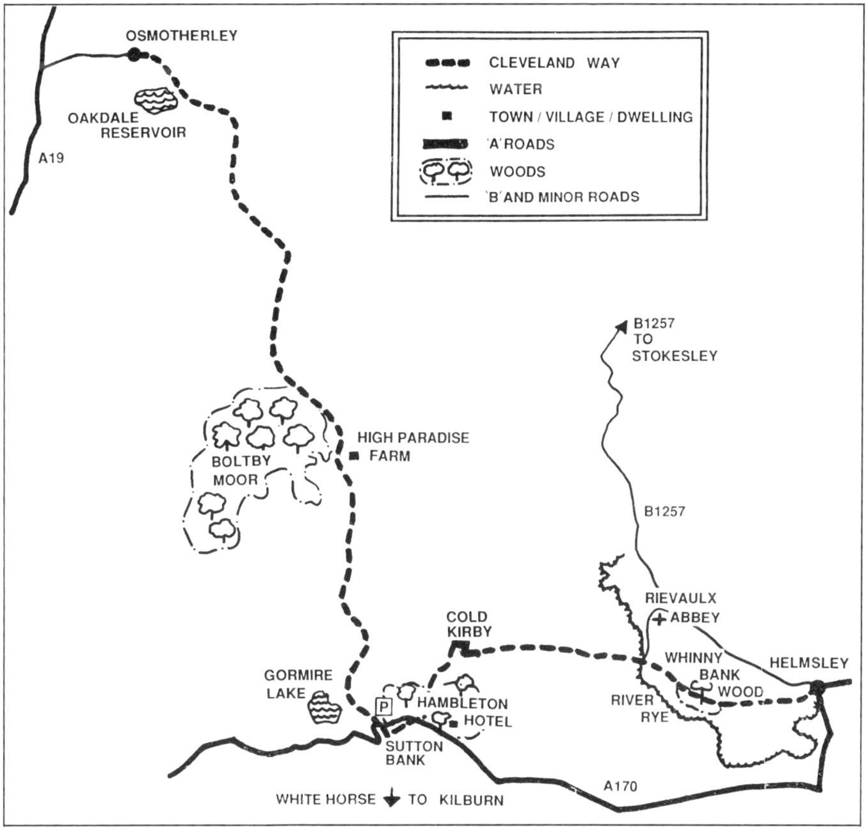

IF, like us, you are doing the Cleveland Way in sections, it's well-worth putting aside a full day for the first eight miles. With Rievaulx Abbey and the famous White Horse at Kilburn requiring only short detours off your track, it is a shame not to include them on the walk. Also, car parks in Helmsley and at Sutton Bank make this an ideal stretch to test out the practicalities of leaving a vehicle at either end, public transport not being what it once was in these parts.

Keen, experienced walkers who take to the countryside to 'get away from it all' will find that somewhat difficult over this initial stage, but don't be put off. There is plenty of opportunity for solitary contemplation further ahead. In the meantime, enjoy sharing your hobby with others — those who don't usually venture too far from civilisation but for whom the three miles from Helmsley to Rievaulx (French for Rye Valley) is feasible.

At least the continuous crocodile of people which winds its way along the field edges in the summer months cannot prevent you from enjoying your surroundings because, quite honestly, they're not that wonderful to begin with. If it's any comfort, had you chosen to walk the Way in an anti-clockwise direction, you would find the scenery of the

The White Horse above Kilburn.

And baby came too ... The Sutton Bank tourist trail.

first few miles out of Filey equally uninspiring.

Even in these environmentally-conscious times, litter is much in evidence, caught in the undergrowth of Blackdale Wood which borders the left side of our path. I hope we are being cynical in suspecting that humans, not the wind, deposited the paper here.

The trail momentarily veers away from farmland and drops steeply into Blackdale Howl where, in a small clearing at the bottom of the dip, sentimentalists will find a Christmas tree graveyard: others will simply see a pile of felled evergreens! No sooner are we down than it's time to climb back up the stepped incline to be faced with unexpected evidence that someone else was here before us. Despite nature's determined efforts to camouflage the remains of a Polish prisoner of war camp, concrete steps and building bases are still clearly visible to the right.

All this unsightliness is instantly forgotten though on emerging from Whinny Bank wood to be confronted with a spectacular view across the Rye Valley towards Scawton Moor. Oh to live in the lodge here at the top of Jinny York Bank and wake up to such an uninterrupted panorama!

The plantation that follows offers welcome shade on a sunny day as the path drops down to meet the road to Rievaulx. There, the Cleveland Way goes straight ahead, over the picture book, hump-back stone bridge. Once essential for carrying traffic over the River Rye on the main route from Helmsley to Sutton Bank, this is now more often used by pedestrians. Two of the most famous must be William Wordsworth and his sister Dorothy who, it is said, once walked from Thirsk to Helmsley en route from their home in the Lake District to see the poet's future wife, Mary Hutchinson, who lived at Brompton on the outskirts of Scarborough.

The creamy-white stone of Rievaulx Abbey half-a-mile away glistens in the sunlight as if beckoning us to take a closer look. If you're a cricket fan and have timed your trip right, you may get no further than the sports field where matches are played in the shadow of the Cistercian ruin, but it is worth a closer look in between innings!

The brotherhood which lived here from 1131 until the 1538 Act of Parliament led to the dissolution of all the country's monasteries, was responsible for the introduction of sheep to the North York Moors. By weaving wool from their flocks, the monks soon had one of the most profitable estates in Europe. To meet the demand for its produce, the original band of 13 French Brothers grew to a 650-strong community well before the end of the century, but first the Black Death in the mid 1300s and then the jealousy and greed of King Henry VIII, who stripped all monasteries of their wealth, put paid to Rievaulx's first residents.

Back on track again and there's another popular, though nowhere near as historic, attraction three miles further on — the Hambleton Inn. The only commercial watering hole directly on the Cleveland Way until Osmotherley, this roadside pub is a very welcome sight.

To reach it, we have passed through the linear village of Cold Kirby (which even on the mildest of days seems to suffer from a fresh breeze and thus live up to its name) and walked within yards of what was once one of Britain's most prestigious race-courses. There are still stables in the area and the Hambleton Downs provide excellent training ground for the horses, but it is almost 200 years since the last race meeting was held here. By then, the most lucrative event — the Hundred Guineas — had been transferred to the York racecourse 20 miles away and Hambleton could no longer draw enough riders to make a meeting viable.

The Hambleton Inn will never be short of punters, especially in the summer when outside tables in the shade and sun cater for all tastes, as does the food. Within minutes of our well-earned rest, we find ourselves on the edge of the Hambleton Hills, gazing into the distance across the Vale of York and trying to recognise landmarks.

It's a stunning view and one you don't quite get from Sutton Bank car park ⅓ of a mile away, even with the help of a strategically-placed telescope. Which explains why our path is crossed by parties who have strayed from

Gormire Lake from the shore's edge.

their touring bus to share our vantage point and take a photograph or two as a reminder of their day out.

At this juncture, things become a trifle confusing. Until now, the waymarking has been wonderfully clear but suddenly, here on the escarpment, we are faced with a choice of direction. According to the wooden signpost, the Cleveland Way is to our left, right and back from whence we have just come! Now, we could toss a coin but, not being one to walk a step further than necessary, I have an aversion to taking wrong turnings and so wisely opt for a spell of map-reading. It turns out that we have arrived at the first of two official Cleveland Way detours. This one offers the opportunity to examine at close-quarters the White Horse on the hillside above Kilburn village.

That incidentally is another place worth a visit when you have time, if only to peep into the workshop of carpenter Robert Thompson. Renowned for his trademark of a little wooden mouse as found, if you look hard enough, on all the pews he has carved in the nearby church, the products of his labour range from bread boards to dining suites and can all be purchased from the adjoining shop — at a price!

As far as we are concerned, a visit there will have to wait, for today the White Horse is as far off the track as we are prepared to go. It puts an extra two miles onto the journey and means doubling back but, recently refreshed and further encouraged by the sight of planes taking off and flying directly above us from the nearby Yorkshire Gliding Club, we can't resist.

We are not alone. For "and baby came to" extend to read "and so did granny and the pet dog". Sutton Bank it seems is THE place to go for a family ramble. Women in high heels try to avoid muddy patches as they struggle to push the baby's pram while fathers keep a tight hold on the toddler's reins — essential if you don't want them to practice their first (and last) free-fall dive off Roulston Scar. A few paces behind comes grandad, walking stick in one hand, dog's lead in the other. This really is a place where there is something for everyone — the gliders (super to watch as they soar in the bright blue sky above Hood Hill, but even more exhilarating to fly which you can do by booking in advance), the bird's eye view of the Vale of York and, of course, the White Horse.

It has to be said that the huge equine shape, infilled with limestone, is best admired from afar. On a clear day (and, I suspect, if you have 20/20 vision) you can apparently see it from the top of York Minster. I'd know if that were true, were I only brave enough to climb the tower! All the same, you really need to walk right up to the horse to appreciate the work that went into its creation by local schoolteacher John Hodgson. He designed it in 1857 and his pupils helped mark it out on the grass slope. But then it took him and 30 volunteers two months to dig out the turf and lime the exposed rock to enhance its whiteness.

The beast is more than 300 feet long and almost 230 feet high and its eye so large that, so tradition has it, 20 people can picnic upon it. Far be it for me to cast doubt on such facts but I fancy it would be a pretty cosy party if that many people turned up. To fit on the eye, they'd all have to be extremely slim and not mind eating while standing up — and very close to each other at that!

Unfortunately we can't test the theory because in order to preserve it polite signs ask sightseers not to tread on the figure, so we head back to Sutton Bank. The 1 in 4 gradient of the A170 road that winds its way up the escarpment does not seem to deter drivers and, even on a wintry weekend, the car park at the top fills rapidly. Also here is a National Park information centre with a well-stocked bookshop, café and public toilets (clean and free!).

If you are calling it a day here, Helmsley is only ten minutes' car drive away. Should you be pressing onwards by foot though, now is your chance to bid farewell to the crowds for you are unlikely to see any again until you reach Osmotherley, 11 miles away. In between is one of the flattest stretches of the Cleveland Way which probably explains why I have such fond memories of this section!

Lift off (hopefully) above Gormire Lake.

Wind-twisted larch trees top Boltby Scar.

The first part of the route takes us along some very steep scars so if you suffer from vertigo, don't look down! Thank goodness the trippers we have just left behind don't realise that the views are equally spectacular on this side of the main road, made especially so by the presence of the only natural lake of any size on the North York Moors.

Lying 500 feet below us at the bottom of Whitestone Cliff, the sparkling calm of Gormire Lake is a sight that will remain with us for the rest of our hike, if not beyond. Described by more than one writer as a "jewel" embedded in Garbutt Wood, it's hard to imagine how it has also become associated with many a morbid legend, some of which have whole communities disappearing into the deep waters, never to be seen again. Such tales may be the result of over-active imaginations but we still take care to watch our step, reluctant to join the horses, riders and even the odd witch who have purportedly taken an unscheduled dive off this very ridge.

Recording historical fact rather than fiction was the goal of archaeologists working in the area during the inter-war period and their efforts did not go unrewarded. Just over a mile away from Gormire, on the site of the Iron Age fort at Boltby Scar, the excavators unearthed a pair of gold ear-rings dating back to the Bronze Age. Unfortunately, the greater part of the hill fort's remains were destroyed by a plough in 1961 and, today, only a low, grass-covered mound and ditch indicate its existence (and even then you have to know what you're looking for to spot them). Anyone interested in ancient history though will enjoy the next few miles for there is more evidence of early settlements further on.

Beyond Boltby Scar, it is a relief to reach a line of dwarf larches under which to sit and cool down before setting off on the last leg of this journey — much of it on the old Drove Road. Just before joining it, we pass through the yard of High Paradise Farm. Three assorted dogs rush out as if to ward us off, but signs offering refreshment to the weary traveller suggest the natives are really quite friendly and we convince ourselves that the ferocious barking is actually "hello and welcome" in canine-speak!

The route we are now following was once used by Scottish and Northumbrian drovers as they moved cattle around the country, although archaeological research suggests the Hambleton Road was used thousands of years before. Tumuli are scattered all over this area and, as you reach the edge of Boltby forest on your left side and come into the open, one of the few long barrows (mass graves) to be found on the moors is just about discernible among the heather.

Cattle has not been seen on the 15-mile long road since the late 1800s when the benefits of rail travel were realised and locally-slaughtered carcasses were sent to market instead of live beasts. Even so, the direct route from Osmotherley to Sutton Bank is obviously still well-used, and not only by farmers driving tractors. Increased usage by the public of four-wheel drive vehicles has left deep ruts in the hard, dry earth, making walking difficult in anything but the thickest-soled shoes. At the time of writing the National Park is investigating the possible ban of such vehicles from the Drove Road.

We've been on the move now for over four hours and each step is becoming more difficult, the track increasingly dusty and the landscape, in parts, depressingly desolate. Only the ruins of Limekiln House hint of an area once busy with lime-burning and stone-quarrying and even that's been uninhabited for nearly a century.

Over the next mile or so the road inclines gently — we'd hardly notice it were we at the start of our day but, now, it seems like we're climbing up to much more than the 1,280 feet that the map shows is the highest point of the Drove Road. The views though of Whorlton and the Cleveland hills (do we really have to climb those eventually?) are worth the trek — but not half as welcome as the sight of the path going downhill towards Oakdale reservoir and on to Osmotherley.

If you can't wait until you reach the village to find a place to eat and drink, Chequers is less than a mile along the road straight ahead. An isolated building with a tall pub-like sign on the green outside, you'll neither be able to miss it nor resist a closer inspection. Its tea rooms offer home-made scones and its farm shop heather honey, free range eggs and game — try fitting all that in your rucksack! There are also camping facilities here. And even if, for some strange reason, the food fails to put a smile on your face, the clever invitation on the wall outside the door certainly will:

"Be not in haste
Step in and taste
Ale tomorrow for nothing"

Think about it before you rush!

Back on course and a quick glance at the map suggests that a lass called Jenny Brewster was most popular in her day around these parts. There's a gill and a spring named after her and it is over the latter we step as we make our way to the reservoir. Depending on who you talk to or which book you read, Jenny takes on various guises, from an innkeeper's wife to a local witch.

A gently-sloping track takes us through the edge of Big Wood, across the lane and over to White House Farm. Only down the valley, over the stream and up Middlestye Bank at the other side — a climb eased by the earthen steps — and at last Osmotherley's parish church tower comes into view. It's amazing how one's pace quickens when the end (temporary though it may be) is in sight!

In a rut on the long, and not-so-winding, Hambleton Drove Road.

Chapter Three

Second Section:

OSMOTHERLEY
TO
CLAY BANK
11.1 miles

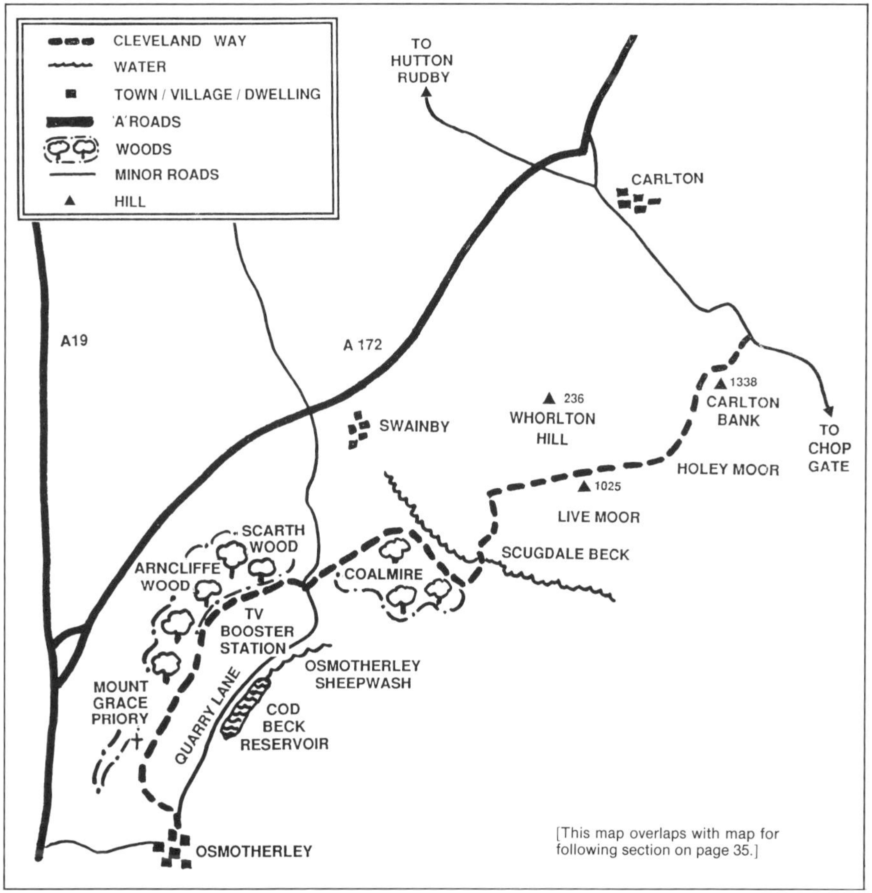

WATER, water everywhere and not a drop to drink ... the rhyme is whirling round and round in my mind as a trickle of water appears out of the undergrowth and tumbles into a ditch while, from the other side of the track, we spy in the distance a stagnant farm pond. We are thirsty — but not THAT thirsty!

Even so, as the sun beats down with increasing ferocity from a bright blue sky, the knowledge that we have only one carton of juice between us is pretty frightening, especially as we are nowhere near the half-way stage of our journey today. Before setting off from Osmotherley, we had taken one car to Clay Bank to await our arrival — it's to be hoped it's a patient vehicle for we are making slow progress in this intense heat. The distance is no more than that between Sutton Bank and Osmotherley but the Cleveland Hills lie between us and our finishing point so, as far as I am concerned, 'home' may as well be on another planet!

To loos – the trek. A relief to arrive in Osmotherley thanks to Ann Cation.

Osmotherley's main street.

We have ahead of us though some incredibly varied scenery and breathtaking views. If only the temperature would drop slightly, it would be the best section of the Cleveland Way. To serious hikers it will be anyway, whatever the weather, and if you have the energy it's worth re-doing at a different time of year, because the change of season can completely alter a view from on high (I know because I was dragged up Cringle and Cold Moor in the snow too!).

Today's soaring temperatures have taken us by surprise. The previous day had been cool and drizzly and a sunhat and plentiful water supply had been the last things on our minds as we packed our supplies. On reflection, we'd have been better sneaking off to the coast and completing a stretch of the walk out of sequence but it's too late now.

It is to be some time before we happen upon an understanding householder who not only revives us with glasses of water but fills up a plastic container to help us along the way. We were lucky — let this be a lesson to other amateur ramblers.

The fact that we are not the only ones in desperate need of moisture is not much comfort. All around is parched. Narrow sandy channels edge the sloping track where once rivulets wound their way downwards; luscious clumps of grass have been replaced by brittle blades and, as we plod along the sandy surface, we kick up dust which settles as a fine film on the nearby shrubs and the backs of our legs. So desert-like are the conditions that I'm expecting Lawrence of Arabia to appear astride a camel at any moment, and even the ice cream van and number nine bus that I spy on the horizon turn out just to be mirages!

We had set off from the pretty village of Osmotherley (referred to as Asmundrelac in the Domesday Book) some hours earlier and, mindful that there's little civilisation along this section of the Way, I'd opted for the 'better to be safe than sorry' routine and popped into the public loos. Normally, I wouldn't consider my calls of nature to be worthy of reference but the afore-mentioned

Easy does it! One step at a time up to Live Moor.

conveniences, tucked behind the parish church, rate as the most unexpected highlight of the hike to date.

A delicate fragrance of fresh flowers had greeted me as I entered the building but it was not these beautiful blooms that caught my eye, nor the homely rug on the spotless floor, but the scores of paper towels strewn around the walls. More often than not the mark of vandals, in this case their presence is attributable to appreciative visitors. Each piece of paper carries a message of thanks to Ann Cation, the lady responsible for keeping the toilets in such pristine condition.

"Tis a pleasure to place your rear" one reads. Elsewhere, the conveniences are described as "wicked", "formidable", "a beautiful experience" and even, according to a group of Nottinghamshire schoolgirls, "edible". They also, adds another, "make you proud to be British". The walls on the Gentlemen's side are equally bright (so I am reliably informed), made so with cartoons, jokes and humorous newspaper cuttings. In return, we don't have to spend a penny. The facilities, open 24 hours a day, are free!

And it isn't just we natives who have appreciated Ann's efforts over the last 25 years. Writers have originated from all over the world. One Australian lady claims the lovely loos have given her a unique memory to take home, while a visitor from Tuscon, USA, invites Ann to go over to America and "show the Yanks what clean is". Could it be that the county's most famous loo lady will be featured in history books along with Osmotherley's central market cross and stone table, once stood upon by preacher John Wesley?

Stand by these on the tiny village green and it's hard to visualise it as the busy industrial centre it once was — Cod Beck on the southern fringe proving ideal to power machinery for cloth weaving and dyeing and the tiny stone cottages providing accommodation for the mill workers and those from the nearby alum quarries and jet mines. Nowadays, with the chance of a job locally practically non-existent, Osmotherley has become a dormitory settlement, ideal commuter territory for those working in the county town of Northallerton or, further north, in Teesside.

There's still a great community spirit though — indicated by the list of groups using the village hall throughout the week and by the existence of three different denomination churches. The Parish one, with its beautiful 15th century porch, hogs the skyline and is impossible to ignore: the Methodist one, not so.

On entering the village through the narrow passage as directed by the Cleveland Way signs, you literally brush past its walls but the noticeboard revealing the tiny building's function is only visible when walking in the other direction. Full marks to anyone who, unlike us, noticed it first time! Catholic masses are held in a church behind the Franciscan friary on North End. The monks here are also responsible for the near 500-year-old Lady Chapel, partly hidden on the hillside above Osmotherley and subject of many pilgrimages every year.

A sign to the chapel accompanies the one directing Cleveland Way walkers northwards out of the village and left along Rueberry Lane. After about half-a-mile, where the track forks, is a slate view indicator, erected by the local civic society in memory of one of its members. It reveals, among other facts, that we are standing halfway between Durham and York, each cathedral city being 30 miles away in opposite directions. Rather closer is the Shrine of Our Lady of Mount Grace and a path that takes you up to it and then drops down to rejoin the Cleveland Way further along.

The earliest evidence of the Chapel's existence is found in a licence for Mass, granted in 1397, but its origins are not known and even its functions in the 15th century are somewhat hazy. The most likely theory is that Carthusian monks lived in it while building their priory at the foot of Mount Grace Hill, from which it took its name. Certainly there used to be steps leading from the monastery to the chapel so the monks could visit the shrine on special days.

The Chapel's later connection with Catherine of Aragon arose when she donated money to enable a

Warm and welcoming. The stately home of Lord and Lady Feversham. *See Chapter 1.*

Winter hits the Cleveland Hills.

Bonny Cliffs, whatever their size, as seen from Carlton Bank.

hermit to live in the building — an act that has gained permanent recognition with the naming of an inn at Osmotherley after the Queen. Even through the Reformation, when Mount Grace Priory was dissolved, the Chapel remained a popular place of pilgrimage and continued in the hands of the Catholic Church until the mid-1800s, after which it fell into disuse and disrepair.

Until, that is, a Yorkshire priest rediscovered it while on a bicycle ride in 1942. Monsignor Peter Storey, now retired and living in Osmotherley, describes his find as the memorable event of his life. "It was a truly exciting moment. The Lady Chapel had been forgotten about except by a few locals," he remembers. That same year, the Chapel was purchased by the Diocese and restored. It re-opened in 1960, since when further building work has been necessary to cope with the increasing numbers of pilgrims. The hermitage is now a Blessed Sacrament Chapel and a small cloister links it to the main place of worship. Its isolation means the complex has to be kept locked but regular services — for example 3.30 p.m. Mass every Saturday — make an internal inspection possible if your visit coincides.

The ruins of Mount Grace Priory — the only Carthusian house in Yorkshire — can also be inspected should you care to take a further deviation from the Cleveland Way. A footpath leads dwn to it from Chapel Wood Farm. The monastery, one of only nine to be founded in England by the silent order, is only half-a-mile away but be warned — you have to climb back up the hillside to rejoin your route at the same point from where you left it.

Our goal from here is the television booster station perched on the edge of Beacon Hill, its unsightliness the price we pay for another popular form of leisure in the 20th century. It's some way off but the fringes of South Wood along which we walk are pleasant enough, save for the constant hum of traffic moving along the A19 down beyond the far edge of the plantation. A triangulation pillar just past the television station marks not only the 981 foot summit of Beacon Hill but the start of the arduous non-stop, 40-mile-long Lyke Wake Walk. We will be sharing the same route for the next ten or so miles, but then I'll leave the hardy hikers to it and stick to our original plan!

As we emerge onto Scarth Moor we are greeted by some of the most breathtaking views — which would be even better if it weren't so hazy. On a clear day, so we are told, you can see across to the Pennines and over Cleveland into Durham. The peaks of Swaledale, Wensleydale and Nidderdale are also visible to the south. For us though, the vast plain stretching into the distance with Swainby village and the gentle shape of Whorl Hill hogging the limelight in the foreground are spectacular in themselves.

The path drops down to meet the Cod Beck valley road. One mile to our right is Osmotherley's Sheepwash — a popular place for a paddle among locals and a nice place for a picnic if you can find a spare patch of grass. Otherwise, the Way takes you over Scarth Nick cattle grid and onto Coalmire. Its name means a cold, marshy place which, at this time of year couldn't be more inappropriate!

The sides of Scugdale valley down to our left were mined for jet in the late 1800s and there is still evidence of the heaps of shale brought to the surface at that time. For close on a mile we walk parallel to the beck that runs along the valley floor until we are led over a farmer's field to a ford that takes us across the water and puts us on the right track for Hollin Hill farm and a row of cottages at Huthwaite Green — the closest we come to civilisation on this section. There is also a telephone box here — a very rare sight on the Cleveland Way.

The wide-spaced wooden steps up the steep slope of Live Moor are a great help — I'll be forever grateful to whoever installed them (an escalator would have been even handier!) for, in this heat with only a handful of grapes to quench our thirst, the going is tough. The traditional mound of stones marks the highest point of the moor but it's some time before I make their acquaintance.

The ruins of Rievaulx Abbey.

Shades of green.

Welcome shade en route to Huthwaite Green.

The sun sets over lovers on Carlton Bank.

And hardly have I time to slump to the ground, than I see another rock pile a few yards on ... and a third in the distance. I keep them in my mind's eye as reachable (just!) targets and before I know it, we've conquered Holey Moor too and are well on our way to Carlton Bank. There, I know, is a gliding club and I keep a close look out for a kind-hearted member who'll lend me his wings to take the weight off my feet but I'm out of luck — not one in sight, only a deserted clubhouse on a barren plateau. Suddenly, out of the heat haze, potential transport arrives. But I blink and it's gone. Father and son cycle past at top speed, hardly a bead of sweat on them, and put me to shame. No more grumblings, I promise as we stagger on. But as I survey the hilly skyline ahead, I wonder how long it will be before I break my vow!

Carlton Bank, described by Bob Cartwright, the National Park's land management officer, as a "scar on the landscape" can, for centuries, hardly have been otherwise. Its current unsightly appearance is blamed largely on motorbike scramblers and, once again, owners of four-wheel drive vehicles. But for over 250 years, alum quarries were excavated here and I can't imagine they were too scenic or kind to the environment either. Even now, decades after the North York Moors alum industry ground to a halt, its mark is clearly visible through the pink coloured shale heaps.

Of great concern though is the moor's rapid erosion. Hopes are high that the National Park can buy the land from its private owner and then instigate remedial action before it's too late. One place where conservation work has already been carried out is on the side of the next hill on our journey — Cringle Moor — at which we arrive after crossing the Raisdale Road and passing a newly built, but unobtrusive, car park, toilets and café. At the foot of the hill is a fenced copse planted in memory of Cleveland Way designer Alec Falconer.

Building drains and heaving heavy wheelbarrows up steep hills isn't everybody's idea of fun but, thanks to the willing workers recruited by the British Trust for Conservation Volunteers, walking up to the summit of

Conquering Wainstones the hard way.

Cringle isn't half as tough on the old muscles as it was last time we were up this way. The young people, from all over Britain, gave up their free time in the autumn of 1990 to do all sorts of essential jobs here, from drain-building to dry stone walling in a bid to halt erosion in its tracks. By the end of 1991, similar repair work, funded largely by the Countryside Commission, had been carried out on the Kirby Bank side of Cringle Moor too.

The working methods, supervised by experts, are traditional but there's no escaping the unnatural newness of the end result. It looks, agreed one of its creators, "like a motorway". But there's no cause for panic because, also on the work brief set out by the BTCV in conjunction with the National Park, is camouflage and the helpers literally sowed the seeds before leaving nature to complete the revegetation process. Within months, few hikers striding up and down the Cleveland Hills will be able to spot that man has lent a protective hand, but it seems ironic that the volunteers' work is only appreciated if it goes undetected!

From the Stokesley to Guisborough road, along which we regularly drive, the Cleveland Hills always look to me like a range of mountains. But then, I'm the type who gets vertigo standing on her front doorstep. Lake District fans on the other hand will no doubt regard Cringle Moor, Cold Moor and Hasty (Norse for horse) Bank as mere molehills compared to their favourite peaks. For me though, the stone seat near the top of Cringle (its peak lies at 1,427 feet but the Cleveland Way doesn't quite go there) makes a welcome change to the carpet of grass upon which I've had to rest up until now. This hiker's armchair enables us to admire the view in relative comfort, aided by a direction indicator placed in front —the second memorial to the afore-mentioned Mr. Falconer Snr.

The mist is thick in the distance and almost obscures the Lowery-esque industrial chimneys of Teesside while, at the same time, leaving us a clear picture of our more immediate surroundings. This is familiar scenery to us but seen from a different perspective and we play spot the local landmarks around Stokesley, Great Broughton, Great Ayton and all the hamlets in between.

Should you require accommodation or merely fancy a drink or two in a quaint old pub then the three larger settlements all offer a choice and are easily accessible from Clay Bank if that is where you have left your car. It might even be worth booking a second night's lodgings in this area for the Cleveland Way Project Officer's survey carried out in 1989 revealed a dearth of places to stay around Kildale which is the next section of the Cleveland Way. Stokesley and Great Ayton especially deserve to be regarded as much more than sites for resting and nourishment.

So proud of their town's history are some of Stokesley's residents that they've formed a society to make locals and visitors alike more aware of what is around them. A large notice-board on the wall of the town hall records important dates and buildings of note. It even suggests a trail that will take you past everything from the 17th century packhorse bridge to the former sites of the once major industries of tallow and linen. I wonder how many folk have raised a wry smile at the irony of the Methodist chapel being on the site of an old pub, the Black Swan, also once the posting house for the Thirsk stage coach.

Great Ayton's origins can be traced back even further through an iron age enclosure up on the nearby moor. Captain James Cook steals the limelight though when it comes to modern history. The fact that he lived in the village as a child is commemorated with a display in the schoolroom, completely separate from the large scale Cook museum in Stewart Park, Middlesbrough. Cook's parents and many siblings are also buried in Great Ayton's ancient parish church cemetery. For the moment though, it is one of the village's other great attractions that I long to see — Suggitt's ice cream, made and sold nowhere else but Great Ayton High Street and the cause of some amazing queues during the summer.

To join them, we must first reach our transport and to do that entails more climbing up hills. As I struggle up

Sun spot.

Evening glow on Cringle Moor's memorial to Alec Falconer.

Solitary and serene above Warren Moor.

Cold Moor on a track that definitely needs to be added to the list of those stretches requiring attention, I feel guilty about promoting the Cleveland Way as a walk that can be enjoyed even by non-hikers. But believe me, if I can do it, anyone can and within seconds of reaching the top, any pain I suffered in doing so (and deservedly for being unfit) is forgotten in the glory of achievement.

Either that, or I have a bad memory for I returned again six months later when, with a slight covering of snow on the highest ground and a chill wind turning my cheek red raw, I still felt the effort was worth it in return for the exhilarating views — of the shaded green Raisdale valley with its scattering of farms in one direction and the Broughton forest plantation immediately below us leading into the plain that stretches as far as the eye can see.

Until summer 1991, the communities nearest to us received their tap water from springs in the hill sides. It sounds refreshing — but not so wonderful during long hot summers when the springs became mere trickles, leaving householders high (well, low actually) and dry. Which is why an underground reservoir was constructed outside Kirkby — the village closest to Cold Moor.

Down we go again, only to face another incline immediately. This time, there's an added incentive to make the upward journey — a closer look at the famous Wainstones. This outcrop of huge boulders is a great practice ground for rock climbers and, even though the Cleveland Way doesn't go directly over them (just as well really as we don't happen to have our ropes and crampons to hand!) scrambling around their edge requires a technique not previously called for on the terrain covered to date.

Ahead of us now, from the plateau of Hasty Bank, we can see clearly the path that the Cleveland Way takes — over the bleakest and highest part of the moor, round to Captain Cook's monument and on to Roseberry Topping. But we will conquer that another day. For the moment, we deserve a break. Clay Bank and a cabin serving take-away snacks awaits us around the corner ... as does a very familiar red Fiesta!

Chapter Four

Third Section:

CLAY BANK TO KILDALE 9.2 miles

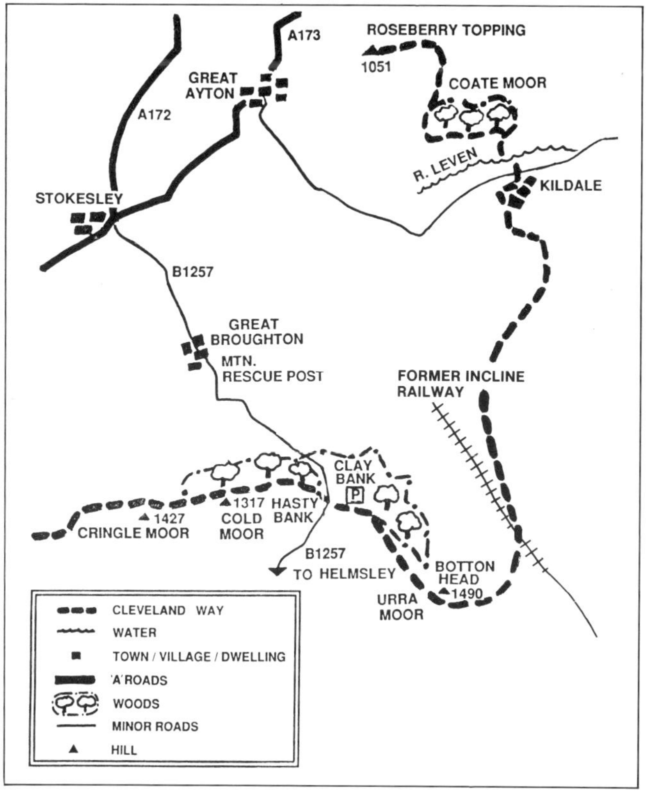

OUR over-riding memory of the first 30 or so miles of the Cleveland Way is one of intense heat. Not so the next part.

Early this morning, the likelihood of bad weather had seemed as remote as the moors we would be crossing but I should have known better than to tempt fate by packing the sun tan lotion!

We sit in the car at Clay Bank, trying to warm up with a cup of hot, steaming coffee, listening to the heavy patter of raindrops as they teem down on to the roof, and hoping that the sky will clear. It doesn't. If anything, the clouds are becoming blacker and heavier.

As soon as we've dug our hither-to unused cagoules from the depths of the rucksack and I have found the motivation to step out into the puddles, we will set off towards the coast, cutting across the North-east corner of the North York Moors National Park.

I'm comforted by the thought that, should the weather deteriorate further and we find ourselves in trouble, help is close at hand. Just down the road in Great Broughton lives Bryan Snowden, chairman of Cleveland Search and Rescue — a 50-strong team of volunteers co-ordinated from his ivy-clad home.

"It's the nearest village to a heavily-used walking area," explains the teacher of humanities, "and I am the nearest member to the hills and a main road." Others live all over Cleveland and North Yorkshire, meaning that wherever the team is called out to, there's always someone on the scene with an intimate knowledge of that area. All are experienced walkers or climbers, trained in a variety of searching techniques and first aid, and wanting to put something back into the pastime from which they've gained so much enjoyment.

In tune with nature. Johanna of the Long Valley.

Captain Cook's monument caps Easby Moor.

On top of the world! Botton Head – the highest point on the Moors.

"Often, they've been in trouble themselves at one time so they know what it's like," says Bryan who has been part of the group since 1965.

Walkers or anxious relatives needing help usually telephone the police who then contact Bryan, either at Weaver's Cottage or at the Middlesbrough school where he works. He then initiates the assembling of team and equipment, the latter comprising largely of stretchers, ropes and a Land Rover.

In 1990, their services were required 14 times. That's 14 times too many of course but a great improvement on previous years, suggesting that people are becoming increasingly more safety-conscious.

"They used to go out into the countryside very badly equipped but that's not the case now," says Bryan. "If people need help these days, it's usually because they've got lost or fallen and failed to turn up to meet someone at an arranged time."

When not combing the countryside in response to an emergency call-out, the search squad's dedicated members can often be found involved in another type of rescue — that of the service itself. Operating solely on donations, a great deal of time is spent fund-raising to keep medical supplies up to date and the four-wheel-drive vehicle on the road. Not only is the team responsible for cover in a 1,000 km^2 area but its assistance is often requested by neighbouring services in the Dales, the Lake District and sometimes, such as after the Lockerbie air disaster, in Scotland too.

And here's me worrying about getting wet! I leap out of the car and negotiate the muddy incline of Urra Moor in what, for me, is no time at all.

As we battle with the elements, we are given great encouragement by the fact that we aren't the only mad fools out on a day like this. On the highest point of the Moors — Botton Head at just under 1500 feet (454m) — we are caught up by a couple of Oxbridge students whiling away their summer vacation by walking the 190-mile Coast to Coast route. Despite the wind and rain lashing around their legs, shorts-clad Jonathan Curry and Mark Rawlings from Stoke are incredibly cheerful and energetic — remarkably so, considering they had completed the Cleveland Way only a fortnight earlier. Obviously not everyone is like I used to be in regarding holidays from education as a chance to relax with my feet up. Ah, those were the days!

No sooner have the two academics left us and disappeared into the distance at a staggering pace, than more figures come into view. I can't believe it — we met hardly a soul when the weather was fine. This time, it's a couple from Essex, led by a very bedraggled Irish Setter called Kelley. A long way to walk your dog, I remark, but Kelley's owners assure us that she loves hiking as much as they do.

By now, my cagoule is as wet on the inside as out and the next layer of clothing is decidely damp too. It isn't always like this up here though. Clumps of purple heather — not usually in flower until the end of August — have been teased by the recent high temperatures into making a premature appearance to line the wayside. White bog cotton waving in the breeze is yet more evidence that summer has been here — it obviously just wasn't prepared to hang around until we arrived.

Only the shrill cry of the lone curlew interrupts the sound of our tramping over the sodden soil. Further on, young grouse flap suddenly out of the shrubbery. Inexperienced at flying, they just about manage to lift their heavy bodies off the floor. "Fly far away," I want to warn them, "in only a few weeks' time, you'll be grounded permanently for the sake of someone's Sunday lunch."

At Bloworth Crossing we finally leave the path we've been sharing with Lyke Wake Walk trekkers since Osmotherley and we turn North along the ancient Rudland Rigg road, originally trodden by travellers going south-east from Fadmoor. If you're a little sneaky, you can actually miss out the crossing (where the old roadway was once bisected by an industrial railway) by taking an earlier path to your left and cutting a corner. This, like one or two other paths in this region, was deliberately created to halt fire in its track. Moorland blazes are incredibly destructive, taking hundreds of hours and men to control, but nature much longer to recover — often all because of a carelessly-discarded match in dry conditions — hence the numerous warning signs all along the Cleveland Way.

The route of the railway is now over to our left. Along it, iron ore was taken from the mines at Rosedale to blast furnaces in Teesside and Durham. From Incline Top, where the foundations of the drum house are still visible, it was gravity which took the laden wagons to the bottom and then a lot of muscle power that brought the empty trucks back up Greenhow Bank. The line was finally taken up in 1928 — eight years after the last load of ore had been transported along it.

As we stride ahead on the top of the bank, the damp

The man to get you out of trouble – Search and Rescue Co-ordinator, Bryan Snowden.

mist is beginning to clear, enabling us to admire the view across the plain of Greenhow Botton (Botton being Nordic for a steep-sided valley) and over towards the Cleveland Hills that we conquered earlier.

For the last few miles, our attention has been captured by the carved stone waymarkers, beginning with the pillar, dating from 1711, on the opposite side of the path to the Botton Head summit cairn. The palm-shape cut into its surface has, not surprisingly, led to it being referred to as a Hand Stone. The Face Stone a little further on has an equally obvious reason for being so-named, although this particular one is thought to originate from Celtic times.

Some are boundary indicators, others direct travellers to towns such as Stoxla (Stokesley), Helmsla (Helmsley) or Pickrin' (Pickering). A few served an even greater function as places where the penniless might find help. Passers-by would leave coins in the indentation on the pillar's peak for more needy people coming along later. We find one today containing a pile of coppers. It's nice to see the tradition continuing but it would be even more helpful if donors took inflation into consideration!

At Tidy Brown Hill, we fork right, off the road that continues to Ingleby Greenhow, and through a gate onto Battersby Moor. Another mile along the open wasteland takes us to the junction with the road to Baysdale, once the site of a small nunnery — Baysdale Abbey — upon which a farmhouse now stands. The rain is now reduced to a fine drizzle and, when the path's surface becomes tarmac, we have little difficulty in picking up pace and making up for lost time, especially on the downward trail from Warren Moor into the tiny village of Kildale.

A post office and a church are about all Kildale has to offer — along with a history dating back to Roman times. Terraces carved out on the steep slopes of Crag Bank are believed to have been created by a Roman farmer. The earliest written proof though of a settlement here is found in a survey carried out in 1086.

This valued Kildale at 20 shillings (£1), indicating it was quite a prosperous community. Firm hopes of making it even more so arose many centuries later when the stone quarrying industry took off on the local moors. A railway station opened in 1858 and business looked like booming. But less than 50 years later, it all came to an abrupt halt when the quarries flooded and predicted profits went down the drain, leaving Kildale to revert to being a sleepy backwater.

The station is still here but that too looks like becoming a relic of the past. The Esk Valley line on which it stands is forever being threatened with closure — the fact that its route from Middlesbrough to Whitby provides passengers with wonderful rural views is not enough to persuade British Rail to keep the line open. If it's still in operation and you fancy a break from walking, it's well-worth setting aside a day to travel the whole length of the route and enjoy the scenery.

For all but the hardy, the last nine miles will have been sufficient to go down on record as a good, substantial day's hike and, unless you were relying on catching a train back to base, you could have done worse than to have left a car at Kildale to take you there. On foot, it's another 14 miles or so to Saltburn and, in that lot, there's Roseberry Topping to climb so it's probably wise to leave that until you're feeling refreshed. That's certainly what we intend doing, given the weather of the last few hours.

Chapter Five

Fourth Section:

KILDALE TO SALTBURN

14.7 miles

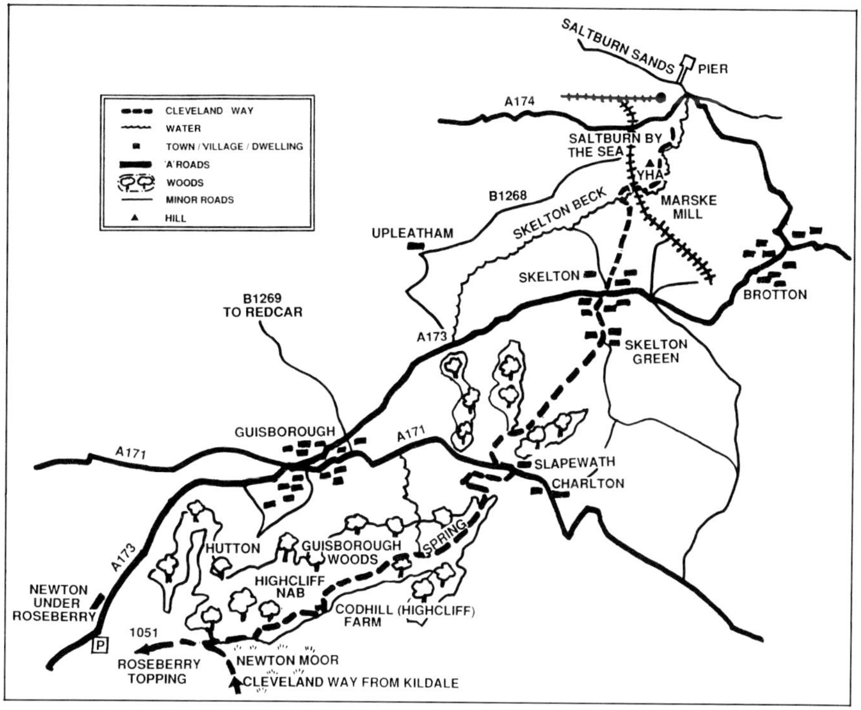

THE Cleveland Way leads off the road to Kildale station almost as soon as we have turned onto it. Had we continued straight ahead, we would also have come to the 19th century church, behind which is the site of a medieval manor, lived in by the Percy family until 1309 when they moved to Alnwick in Northumberland. It remained, however, in their ownership until 1660 when it was bought by a John Turner. Two members of the Percy family are buried here and Percy Cross Rigg across Lonsdale Valley is another permanent reminder of the clan's local connections.

Having crossed the River Tees' longest tributary, the River Leven (its name a derivation of the Welsh 'Leuan' meaning water nymph) and emerged from the woodland, we are presented with a picture to our left of the village church sitting high on the opposite bank. Away in the other direction is the Esk Valley, obliterated from sight by undulating farm fields. Soon after passing Bankside Cottage which offers Bed & Breakfast, and a farm of the same name, we are deprived of any view whatsoever as, for the next mile, we make our way through the middle of Lonsdale Forest.

If it's the right time of year and you were observant enough, you may have noticed clumps of violets growing in the hedgerows that line the track from Kildale to the forest's entrance. Although in their natural habitat, many of these pretty flowers would not be here were it not for the efforts of a local lady intent on "enhancing the walk" and, more importantly, on saving England's wild plant species.

"When I walk and I look and I find a rare plant, I am so delighted that I want to tell everyone because all the species are dying out and unless people are considerate to them, the next generation will not know them," we are told by a very passionate, white-haired but youthful septuagenarian as we sip coffee in her cosy, cluttered sitting room.

Johanna ("call me Johanna of the Long Valley if you must have a surname") lives isolated but never lonely in a former farmhouse on the northern edge of the Coate Moor. Here, she has transformed a barren patch of ground into an idyllic cottage garden where plants are grown for their medicinal qualities as much as anything. She may pick some comfrey and make an ointment to soothe bunions, infuse leaves of the yarrow to help ease symptoms of fever, or pick some plantain to make a medicine renowned for arresting internal bleeding. Herbal medicine, Johanna advocates, should be considered as a companion to traditional treatments rather than as an alternative.

"Everything has a cure. I have made a collection so there is always something here for people who need it," says this altruistic woman in her soft, Welsh voice. "I want plants to survive but, most of all, I want people to survive."

We don't have any ailments for Johanna to cure but we go on our way feeling all the better for an hour's conversation with such a delightful and enthusiastic eccentric, known jokingly to her friends as "The White Witch!"

As we emerge from the forest at its western fringe, it's impossible to miss our next port of call — the 60-foot-high memorial to Cleveland's most famous son, the sea-faring Captain James Cook. We've seen the stone monument silhouetted in the distance from various points en route and, I have to confess, there were times when I never thought I would actually reach it. But here we are at last, close enough if not actually to touch it (protective railings prevent that), to read the attached plaque.

It explains how the obelisk was erected in 1829 by Robert Campion of Whitby and restored before the turn of the century by readers of the *North East Daily Gazette*. The dedication describes Cook as "A man in nautical knowledge inferior to none: in zeal, prudence and energy, superior to most" and goes on to explain how his massacre in Hawaii on February 14th, 1779 caused "inexpressible grief to his countrymen".

You may not have been aware of Cook's origins before you set out on the Cleveland Way but you will be a near expert on his life story by the time you have finished! This monument on Easby Moor is the first of three reminders of his Cleveland/Yorkshire connections that you will come across, others being at Staithes and Whitby, and there are plenty more if you are interested enough to deviate slightly and follow the Captain Cook Heritage Trail devised by local tourist chiefs. It leaves me wondering just how far an area's pride in its links with a famous historical character can go before exploitation takes over and has a counter-effect.

There are lots of paths leading to and from the monument, proving what a favourite focal point it is for a family ramble, and we pass a cluster of cars and their picnic-partaking occupants at Gribdale Gate as we cross over the road and work our way up Ayton Bank. Between here and Roseberry Topping, the trail is not just flat but often downhill and I even break into a canter at one stage. It's such a shame that Simon can't keep up to capture the occasion on film for no-one will ever believe that I'm capable of moving faster than a snail!

Mind you, my out-of-character speed doesn't last long — the sight of Roseberry Topping's steep sides soon wipes the smile off my face. We don't have to climb it for it's not directly on the route, but gives rise to the second and last official detour, and even I can't resist the challenge of Cleveland's very own 'Matterhorn'.

Although only just in the mountain category at 1057 feet (320m), Roseberry Topping appears higher because

Sledging on the slippery slopes of Great Ayton Moor.

the land around it is so flat. You can see it from miles away and even the most un-athletic are drawn to investigate the unusually-shaped peak at close-quarters. Mind you, it hasn't always looked as it does now — covered in vegetation, save for a rough section of rock to the South-west of its summit.

Its current features can be blamed on iron-mining subsidence in 1907, as recalled by pensioner Arthur Cumbor, for more than 90 years a resident of Great Ayton where he is referred to simply as AK: "We thought the world was coming to an end," he says of the landslip. "Shortly afterwards, a young boy tried to climb down the side of the fallen rock and was killed." A much happier memory of Roseberry Topping for AK, and certainly his first, is of seeing a bonfire on the top, lit to celebrate the coronation of Edward VII.

Back in Viking times, the hill was known as Odinsbergh. This was altered slightly in 1119 to Othensberg and from that became Ouesbergh, with the village at its foot being known as Newton under Ouesbergh. Eventually, the letter 'R' was added to the beginning. The subsequent inheritance of today's name is obvious.

The influence of Roseberry Topping on the local community can be traced back beyond history into legend. The most famous of these involves a baby Saxon prince. The child's mother was told that her son, Oswy of Northumbria, would drown on a specified day so she took him to the summit of Roseberry Topping as far away as possible, so she thought, from water. But just below the peak was a well (or, in some versions, a spring) in which, sure enough, the prince drowned.

Back to reality and, in the 19th century, like much of the surrounding land, the mountain was mined for both jet and ironstone. Now though, it's owned by the National Trust and exists solely as a landmark much appreciated by walkers and passers-by.

Whatever the time of year or day, you will always see vehicles in the car park at the bottom of Roseberry Topping. If you are leaving your motor here before setting off on a day's hiking, it is reached by going along the A173 Stokesley to Guisborough road. There are also public toilets and, only yards away in the exclusive village of Newton, the chance of a wonderful meal at the Kings Head. It is only a chance though because, such is the pub's gourmet reputation that, unless you've booked in advance, you'll be lucky to find a seat. Not to worry though, the next stretch of the Cleveland Way passes nearer to civilisation than did the whole lot that we've covered to date so the opportunity to eat will never be far away.

Guisborough, the ancient capital of Cleveland, is only an hour's walk from here but that's plenty of time in which to work up an appetite. We certainly did. But then we walked twice as far as we needed to, passing as we did through these parts before a survey directed the attention of Cleveland Way Project Officer, Ian Keirle, to the lack of acorn-daubed signposts.

Since then, they seem to have appeared on almost every tree trunk! "If anything, we have gone too much the way of caution," Ian admits. "But you will find it very difficult to get lost in the woods now." Which is great news for unskilled map-readers who might otherwise have followed in our footsteps and accidentally wandered through Hutton Woods instead of over Hutton Moor. Thankfully Highcliff Nab is a prominent enough rock outcrop to spot from a distance and we were able to get back on the right track.

Not that Hutton Woods aren't to be recommended, but another time perhaps! We enjoyed them so much — the warm sun making welcome appearances in the occasional clearance and the frequent flap of wings as birds of all sizes were scared off by our sudden imposition on their territory — that it was 15 minutes before we even realised we'd gone wrong. It was the total absence of other people that finally alerted us for, going by the numbers we'd passed on Newton Moor at the back of Roseberry Topping, we knew this was a popular corner of Cleveland.

There'd been the energetic trio of Guisborough school

pupils cycling across the fell as part of their outdoor-pursuits lesson (whatever happened to the Rugby in Winter: Cricket in Summer syndrome?). And not long afterwards, we'd passed the time of day with three German hikers who'd set out from Filey five day's previous to complete the Cleveland Way in reverse, spending the nights under canvas.

The correct trail goes around the back of Highcliffe Farm. Don't let any old signs to Codhill Farm confuse you — they're one and the same place, the latter being its original name.

Not being too keen on heights, I wouldn't have liked to climb the grassy bank to Highcliff Nab without the aid of the steps there and, once on top, I had no intention of going close to the edge. There was no need. The spectacular aerial view of Guisborough and right across the rooftops to the coast can be enjoyed without risking life and limb. It's like looking down on Legoland — all the tiny houses, interspersed with smooth green squares of playing fields, forming the post-war estates that have transformed Guisborough from a rural market centre to a dormitory town for employees of such major companies as ICI and British Steel on Teesside. Rising above it all though, as we trace the tree-lined main street to our far right, are the ancient remnants of Gisborough Priory.

The Cleveland Way continues along the top of Highcliff Wood until it comes to a spring when it begins to drop down gently. Your cue to turn off down into Guisborough town centre comes 600 yards on, when the path forks — right for the Cleveland Way; left for refreshments, shops and a splash of historical culture should you so desire.

To reach the latter, just keep to your chosen course even when the surface becomes paved. You'll know you've arrived when you bump into the recently restored market cross which, with its colourful sundial and shining weather vane, perches on an island surrounded by busy roads. To reach it, you will have walked down Belmangate, the correct name for which is Bellemond Gate — 'entrance to the pleasant world'. When you return from town towards the fields and tree-covered slopes to rejoin the Cleveland Way, you will appreciate how apt the name is.

Originally Belmangate was a drover's road along which medieval townsfolk took their animals to and from the moor. Later, it was used by monks as a highway from Rosedale Abbey to Gisborough Priory and then, in the 17th, 18th and 19th centuries, it was a vital link between the town and mines in the hills, first alum workings and then ironstone.

History and tradition is rife in the town too, where for 600 years market traders have set up stalls on the cobbles of the main thoroughfare. The Priory's roots go back even further although, with only the Norman-style archway still standing, you'll need some sound architectural knowledge and a vivid imagination to envisage it in all its glory. It was founded in 1119 by Robert de Brus, who belonged to a branch of the Bruces who ruled Scotland, and became one of the wealthiest Augustinian monasteries in the country. Having twice been destroyed by fire, the ruins are of a church built in the early 14th century. Now in the custody of English Heritage, the stone structure and surrounding gardens are well-cared for and open to the public all year round.

The priory dominated Guisborough (burgh being a defended settlement; Gigr a Scandinavian name) since it owned all the land round about — a responsibility adopted these days, albeit on a somewhat smaller scale, by the county's Lord Lieutenant, Lord Gisborough (like the priory and the moor, no 'u' in his name) who lives in part of the converted stable block at Gisborough House just out of the town on the Whitby road.

Ten years after the Dissolution of the Monasteries, the land was bought by Thomas Chaloner who systematically demolished all the Priory buildings to create room for his own luxurious residence to be built. The town remained largely agricultural until the 1850s when ironstone mines were opened on Belman Bank and at nearby Slapewath and rail links connected Guisborough

Salt of the earth ironstone miner, George Johnson.

first to Middlesbrough and later, in the opposite direction, with Skelton. The whistle was finally blown on the local railway network in 1964 when the Beeching axe fell and there is now a health centre where once Guisborough station stood.

There's lots more worth mentioning but if you're on your way to Saltburn, you won't have much time to look around. However, a visit to Guisborough museum will sum up everything for you in one go. It's not a traditional one full of showcases but a room full of memorabilia — costumes, shop fittings and household objects from bygone days — all donated to local estate agent Roger Darnton who has put them together on display so that others can find pleasure in his private collection. Situated behind Sunnyfield House on Westgate, the museum is open from 10 am to 4 p.m. on market days — Thursday and Saturday.

Having given Guisborough a miss this time, we press on to arrive at the Fox and Hounds in Slapewath for lunch and are shaded for much of the journey by Guisborough Woods. Spread over nearly 200 acres of the north-facing escarpment, the forest comprises mainly coniferous trees, planted after the Second World War to offset cheap timber imports and to create local employment. Government pressure is now being put upon the Forestry Commission to add recreation to these 'reasons for being' by introducing picnic areas, walkways and even an information centre. But such schemes, should they ever take off, will still remain of secondary importance to timber production.

With only seven homes in Slapewath, the Fox and Hounds Hounds obviously isn't going to generate profits from local trade but the road passing only yards away is the main route from Teesside to the coast and motorists seem to keep pub staff busy. We added our contribution to the coffers in seeking much-needed refreshment before attempting the final climb of this section — up Spring Bank.

It doesn't seem half as bad as it might have done without a couple of glasses of orange juice inside us and the way from now on seems pretty easy going. Down Airy Hill Lane to Skelton Green we stride and on the footpath towards Skelton itself. Looking beyond the ever-growing parish, before dropping down to it, Skelton Castle is clearly visible, more than holding its own in the modern community despite being eight centuries old.

Built by Robert de Brus (he of Gisborough Priory), the house has remained in the ownership of his ancestors ever since, passed on through marriage, succession and family settlement. Its present occupant, Major Tony Wharton, inherited the estate of 10,000 acres and 150 let properties in 1991 on the death of his 96-year-old cousin, Margaret Ringrose-Wharton, and is the 31st generation of the family to own the castle.

In the other direction, and not too far in the distance, we can see today's destination — Saltburn. Before reaching it though, we undergo an enormous culture shock. First of all, there's Skelton High Street to be negotiated with all its shops and heavy traffic, the likes of which we have not before encountered on the Cleveland Way. And then we find that the path actually takes us through a modern housing estate. The sound of walking boots clumping on paving slabs is difficult to come to terms with at this stage in the game. As for following the sign of the acorn from lamppost to lamppost well, whatever happened to the rural landscape about which I have been enthusing since Day One?

Mind you, it's not that long ago since people passing through this district would have found themselves almost surrounded by ironstone mines, the Skinningrove valley just down the road being the site of the original workings of Cleveland's main seam and North Skelton being the last to be worked, closing in 1964.

The final blast there was fired by miner George Johnson who has lived in the same house in Skelton since 1940. "I put all the supports up and drilled the holes. The following day, a film crew came in and I fired the last shot. It was like a big cannon going off," he remembers. As far as George knows, the resulting 20 ore-filled tubs have never been brought to the surface, remaining underground — a tribute to him and those like him who devoted, and sometimes lost, their lives to the development of East Cleveland.

"It wasn't all honey and sugar down there, you know," George points out in his broad Yorkshire accent. But he dismisses in an instant, details of the roof collapse that saw him buried up to his waist and left him badly crippled in old age. "I would do it all again if I could," he grins.

We could spend all day listening to George's first-hand accounts of a world so remote from today's hi-technology but, wishing to see Saltburn in the daylight, we leave him drawing contentedly on his pipe in the company of his beloved pet dog, Rick, and we take to the road again. Only Crow Wood and Skelton Beck now lie between us and the North Sea. Never again on these travels will we be so far inland but we are looking forward to yet another change of scenery when we begin to tackle the 42-mile coastal stretch of the Cleveland Way.

Roseberry Topping – Cleveland's very own Matterhorn.

Chapter Six

Fifth Section:

SALTBURN TO SANDSEND 17.2 miles

"THE JEWEL in the crown of Cleveland's coastline" is a description of Saltburn that's been used more than once in recent years and not without justification. There's still some way to go before the Victorian town is in the running for the title of Queen of East coast resorts but, if changes in the next decade are as dramatic as those in the last, it won't be long before it reigns supreme.

A combined effort by the community and Langbaurgh, the local authority, with help from EEC funds has resulted in a change of face for Saltburn. Tourism is very much the buzz word but not to the detriment of its reputation as a desirable place to live.

There is no greater evidence of this than during the annual Victorian Festival when the citizens put on a spectacular show that they themselves enjoy as much as the visitors. For one week in August, local people, young

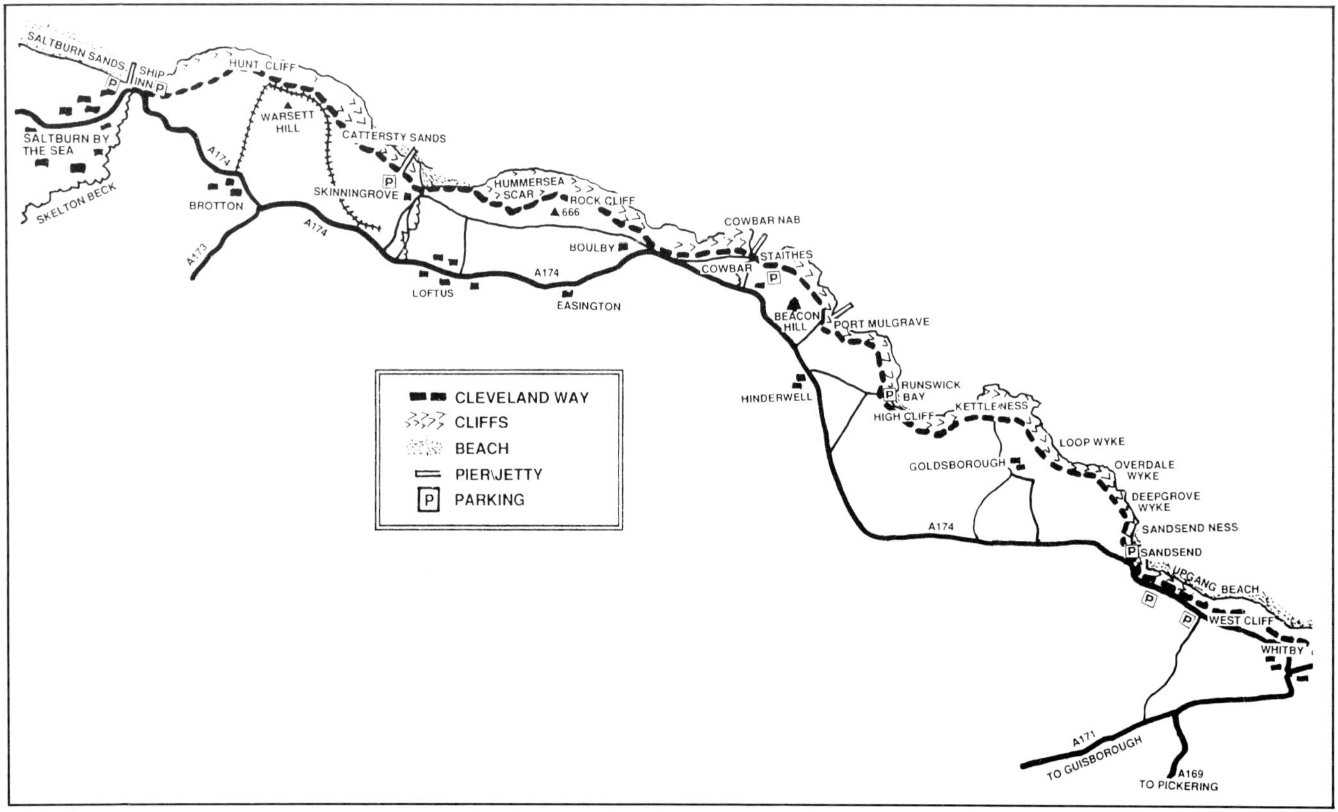

and old, trader or customer, go about their daily business dressed in period costume. With much of the town still retaining its original appearance and many such features having been recently restored, it isn't difficult to imagine you've stepped back in time ...

Back in fact to the late 19th century when Darlington woollen mill-owner, Henry Pease, made the first moves to really put Saltburn on the map. Taking a walk in the area one day, he claimed to have experienced a prophetic vision of "a town arisen on the edge of the cliff" and the "quiet unfrequented glen turned into a lovely garden".

Fact or fantasy, the entrepreneur's foresight resulted in the transformation of a community comprising largely of fishermen and smugglers into Saltburn-by-the-sea, a popular Victorian holiday resort.

Pease formed the Saltburn Improvement Company (SIC) which went on to instigate the construction of new houses for incomers and the Zetland Hotel for visitors; the provision of drains and roads; a place of worship; and, much later, the brine baths, the pier and a bridge across the glen. Known as the Ha'penny Bridge, it was demolished in the early '70s.

Henry Pease's achievement in creating a town from virtually nothing was remarkable and rapid: its demise after his death was almost as fast. His creations were maintained but not improved and it was to be another 90 years before people began to care as much about the local environment as he did.

Saltburn Residents is the SIC's modern day equivalent — an umbrella organisation for a myriad of smaller groups all anxious to boost the appearance and morale of their home town. There's the 500 Club for example, formed in 1989 by people with the common aim of raising money to benefit their environment. The hundreds of pounds collected in its first couple of years bought litter bins, Christmas lights and bunting for carnival week — "anything for the good of the town really," explains Club member Audrey Boagey — but ultimately their aim is to build a new bandstand. Sunday concerts are still held during the summer in Saltburn but

Stepping back in time, during Saltburn's Victorian Festival.

Guisborough Priory.

Springtime at Skelton Castle.

Spectrum after the storm over Saltburn Pier.

they've never sounded quite the same since the disappearance of the bandstand from the pleasure ground.

Also thriving are an arts society that has a while since celebrated its silver jubilee, an active drama group called the '53 Society after the year in which it was formed and The Victorians, keen to revive those heydays of the mid-1800s and the enthusiasts behind the Victorian Festival. In short, Saltburn's community spirit is now at its height.

Having been a resident for over 40 years, Audrey Boagey remembers the days when Saltburn was derelict and living here was not something to boast about. "But now it's such a good place to be. The whole town is just revitalised — it's marvellous. Saltburn is on the map again — and I don't just mean the Cleveland Way map."

Which makes it difficult to understand the Youth Hostel Association's decision to close its Saltburn premises in the summer of 1991 — 54 years after it was presented to the YHA by the King George V Memorial Trust.

After this lengthy indulgence in nostalgia, we make our way to the Ship Inn at the southern end of the beach for it is there that we pick up the Cleveland Way trail again. From the town centre, this means going down the famous Saltburn Bank and gives us an excuse to ride in the cliff lift. Opened in 1884, it's the oldest water-balance cliff railway in Britain and runs directly above Saltburn's pier. This isn't a very long structure but at least it's still standing, having resisted both wave erosion and man's moves to demolish it because of repair costs, which is more than can be said for the majority of the country's piers!

The lift is not just a novelty but a great energy-saver — as you'll discover if you visit Saltburn out of season when the lift isn't in operation and you have to walk up and down the bank, this being either a windy or steep trek depending on whether you choose to go via the road or the steps. If you have arrived by car to begin your hike, such exertion is unnecessary as there are two car parks on the lower level promenade, as well as one at the Ship Inn.

Before we begin our climb, for that is what is immediately required if we are to get onto the top of the cliffs that gave Cleveland (land of Cliffs) its name, we'll just nip inside the pub — not to indulge, you understand, but to investigate its smuggling connection.

Smuggling was rife in Saltburn for a couple of centuries, with the main instigator being John Andrew, landlord of the Ship Inn towards the end of the 18th century. When he'd made his fortune, Mr. Andrew bought the White House at the top of the hill and, in 1966, workmen supposedly discovered a tunnel leading there from the hostelry.

After the Napoleonic Wars, smuggling became unprofitable but the life and illegal dealings of Mr. Andrew still fascinate, and form the focus of a new museum situated in converted cottages adjoining the Ship Inn. Trade at the pub may have changed direction these days, but it remains as good as ever. Customers visit from all over the world and, with a ship wheel in one bar, a figurehead from a wrecked vessel in another and local cod the highlight of the menu, there's no getting away from its links with the sea. But it's not just a tourist attraction: fishermen frequent The Ship too. And farm labourer Les Jefferson, who enjoyed his first sup of beer in the back bar at the age of 16, is still a regular in his seventies.

Today, he's holding audience with four New Zealanders on the last leg of their world tour. They've had lots of adventures but find Les's tales of old Saltburn as fascinating as any.

"At yon end of the fishermen's bar were old biscuit tins and crab pots. They used to burn seaweed on the fire. You went in there and the smoke hung in the air," he remembers. Over one corner of the bar, a paraffin lamp had hung on a nail, dripping oil and adding a unique flavour to the beer if you happened to leave your glass in the wrong spot. "I got my first-ever beer and complained it tasted of paraffin — they gave me a second pint free!" laughs the old man.

In those days, Saltburn comprised about 130 houses at

A charming sculpture on Hunt Cliff.

Skinningrove Beck – a lasting reminder of the ironstone industry.

Bonnets and bairns – the traditional Staithes costume lives on.

Sunbeams fight their way through the chimney smoke above Staithes.

Boulby potash mine dominating the skyline.

the top of the bank while, at the bottom, were four cottages by the pub, the old mortuary and lifeboat station across the way and a farmhouse on the other side of the beck. Half the pub was a coach-house for it was a well-known wayfarers' arms.

"Saltburn's changed — and not for the better," Les claims. "They blew up the ha'penny bridge ... and half the pier. The station was splendid but you can't bring those things back — no matter how many Victorian Weeks there are. You can't make it what it was."

Les is happy to talk all day, provided he has a pint in his hand and his dog Daisy lying lazily at his feet. But we have a job to do, so we bid the genial gentleman farewell and set off up to the coastal path which is to become familiar territory for many hours.

This is the part of the walk I've been waiting for. I have this vision of sun, sea and sand for 50 miles and it's the only thing that's kept me going on some of the steeper stretches. The track is easy to follow, rarely straying from the cliff edge and creeping ever-nearer to it as erosion takes its toll. I wouldn't like to be up here when the ground is wet for we have to be pretty sure-footed in places and it can't be long before the path has to be moved a few yards inland for safety's sake.

Looking back from Hunt Cliff, we have a fabulous view of the whole of Saltburn — and the not so wonderful sight of industry-infected Teesside. Now I know why the Cleveland Way experts suggest we do the walk in a clockwise direction, putting such sights behind us.

It's also easy to appreciate why the Romans chose to put a signal station up here as an early warning system to their North-east coast fleets. Thought to have been constructed in AD 367, mass erosion has seen to it that only a ditch and defensive wall remain, although an excavation in 1911 turned up the remains of 14 people, a leather sandal and two bowls.

To our right at this time is the mineral railway line serving Boulby potash mine, and the Guibal fan house which used to ventilate Huntcliff mine when it was in production between 1872 and 1906. This monument to the ironstone industry retains some of its original fittings, which help to explain how the fan operated, and make it one of the best-preserved examples of its kind in the country. But for most of our way we are flanked by farm fields, many in the throes of harvest.

A farmer's plan to diversify by turning some of this agricultural land into a golf course was turned down pretty sharply in 1990, but served a purpose in alerting countryside lovers to the fact that 150 acres of Hunt Cliff were privately owned and its future therefore lay in the hands of a few individuals. This prompted a move by the National Trust to buy the land as part of its Enterprise Neptune scheme and hundreds of members answered the call for £25 donations (the equivalent of one foot of cliff) to help raise the £50,000 needed for the NT to own its first stretch of Cleveland coastline. One that is home to colonies of gulls, cormorants and eider ducks and rich in orchids, thrift and a variety of plants.

It is also, to the delight of some, and horror of others, the site of three steel sculptures, designed and made by Hampshire artist Richard Farrington to reflect the local environment and community. "They are my reaction to it, not my interpretation — I don't like that word," he insists.

Thus the first two, placed close to each other on the headland and easily missed if you're concentrating on your way ahead at the time, are symbolic of the importance to man of the sea and the elements. One, representing a fish in a trawl door (used by fishermen to keep the nets open) is partially hidden in an overgrown hollow: the other, a column of track steel from which a chain of symbols leads to the ground, stands above on an earth mound and calls for a few yards deviation if curiosity gets the better of you.

There are no explanatory notices to hand — both the sculptor and Cleveland Arts, which commissioned him as part of the national New Milestones Project, preferring on-lookers to use their imagination. Which is all very well if you have one! I'm not sure that I have, for these metallic monsters leave me cold. The last one, however,

Picturesque Runswick Bay.

Dawn breaks over Kettle Ness.

on the trackside half-a-mile away and impossible to ignore, is far more appealing to the eye and, now I know the thinking behind its creation, much more meaningful too.

After enlightenment, the black steel circle with ten seemingly unrelated objects hanging from it becomes an oversized bracelet with each charm representing an aspect of local life. There's a Cleveland Bay horse for example, a starfish and piece of seaweed, a pigeon (fancying being a traditional East Cleveland sport) and a cat after CatNab — the native name for the conical hill opposite the Ship Inn that separates Skelton Beck and Saltburn Gill.

Other walkers it seems are able to translate without help or even appreciate it without knowing the background. John Young and Brenda Desborough, out on an afternoon's stroll, had approached the circle from the opposite direction to us and seen it from some distance, silhouetted against the deep blue sky.

"This is wonderful," says John as he takes hold of the owl shape. "It represents the area where I was born and the skills of the people. It's strong, it's bold and it's raw." Brenda admits she isn't usually attacted to sculpture but, this time, she has to agree with John. "This is absolutely brilliant," she says.

Landscape gardener Chris Humphrey, on his way to Whitby, is a little more cautious in his initial reaction, especially with regard to the first two sculptures. "Unusual" and "interesting" being the adjectives which he admits spring to mind. "It's all very symbolic, but aesthetically they don't mean a lot," he adds. For the circle though, with its charms clanging together in the breeze, he awards nine points out of ten!

A farmer working nearby gives his opinion also, disguised in a brief philosophical comment that says it all: "Like they say, it's all in the eye of the beholder isn't it? They've stimulated a lot of thought though and if they get people down here then that's alright."

We leave him studying the sculptures with a somewhat bemused expression on his face and, as the freight line turns away inland, we get our first glimpse of what we've been longing for since Helmsley all those miles ago — a long and near-deserted sandy beach onto which gentle waves are lapping ashore. It doesn't take us long to work our way through the dunes and dabble our toes in the icy water.

Had I known what was on the other side of the jetty, I wouldn't have been so keen. I've never been to Skinningrove before and can't contain my horror when we round the corner from Cattersty Sands to see bright orange water flowing down the gully into the sea. Once a tiny fishing hamlet, Skinningrove underwent a dramatic transformation in the mid-1800's when industrialists recognised the potential of the newly-discovered thick ironstone seams in the valley. Within 40 years, the community had increased almost thirty-fold from 63 to 1,775 (most of whom were male) and the traditional stone and clay pantile cottages were replaced by brick and slate terraced houses.

The ironstone was originally taken by tramway to the beach and loaded from the jetty onto ships going to blast furnaces on the River Tees or Tyne, but an extension of the railway brought a better alternative means of transport to the valley. This was also the final factor in turning Skinningrove into a mini-Middlesbrough or, as Bill Cowley suggests in his 1969 book on the Cleveland Way, "paradise into an inferno". Nowadays, it's neither. The beck is still discoloured by iron oxides but only the British Steel works perched on the top of Cattersty Cliff betray the area's industrial past and, there too it is fading, with steel being brought in from elsewhere to be rolled. Even the houses have been rebuilt, though still in unimaginative rows, and their occupants tend pigeons on the very hillsides below which their predecessors once grafted.

It is in recognition of and admiration for the latter that local journalist Tom Leonard collected relics and photographs of East Cleveland's ironstone industry. After Tom's death in 1981, his family and friends created a museum in his memory. The result of their efforts is the

Early morning in Staithes Bay.

Clem James – Staithes bred, but not born.

Cowbar Nab from the Staithes side of the harbour.

Tom Leonard Mining Museum which stands at the western end of Skinningrove on the site of the former Loftus mines and is open every afternoon from Easter to October. The old engine house is now the museum's entrance hall and, from there, we walk through the fan house and along the ventilating drift to experience for ourselves the cold, damp and dark conditions in which the miners worked.

It's nice to get back out into the fresh air and sunshine and pick up the Cleveland Way again. Once up on Hummersea Cliff, the view of Skinningrove is soon blocked from view by the second Warsett Hill we have come across today — the first being just this side of Hunt Cliff.

Having left behind evidence of one geologically-based industry we soon come face to face with the residue of another. Sandstone-capped quarries to our left and sloping shale faces, so windswept that vegetation is unable to establish itself, still dominate the landscape even though it's over a century since the area was last worked for alum. From 1650 until then, Boulby had been the centre of the country's main alum producers —alum being used as a fixative in cloth dyeing as well as in the tanning of leather and paper making. The derelict quarries don't make a pretty sight and we concentrate instead on Boulby's more impressive claim to fame — at 666 feet (203m), its cliff is the highest on the East coast of England.

Dropping down steeply from Rock Cliff, the path returns to the land's edge for a short spell before taking us through Boulby and past another landmark which, as far as hungry and thirsty hikers are concerned, is by far the most important. The last in a row of cottages is known as Walker's Halt and, here, passers-by are welcomed — muddy boots 'n all — into the home of Eric and Nina Hibbin.

To the couple who retired here from Tyneside, serving up hot mugs of tea and snacks such as beans on toast and even tending blisters has become a way of life.

"We live in an isolated place and we now have company," Nina explains. "We used to walk a lot ourselves and know from experience and the stories we get from visitors that a day is made by the reception given at stopping off places."

Which is why 'Mr. and Mrs. Not-too-much-trouble' (as one letter of thanks was addressed) have rebelled against hostelries and guest houses that ban boots, rucksacks and the eating of one's own food by displaying notices to the contrary. And judging by comments in the visitor's book and the tales Eric and Nina recount, such friendly gestures are warmly appreciated.

"We don't like too much publicity," says Nina. "We like to keep this place as a surprise for walkers. They have just climbed the highest cliff on this side of England and think they are in the middle of nowhere. Seeing us is a kind of mirage!"

Such is the Hibbins' sense of responsibility towards the well-being of long-distance walkers that they even feel guilty about going out and having to put up the closed sign. But they admit that it is nice occasionally to spend a few uninterrupted hours, just the two of them in the cosy cottage, so we take the hint and press on towards Staithes where we have an appointment.

Immediately, we pass the site of the alum house —now a swimming pool — where the crystallising process took place. The house next to it was once a warehouse for sacks of crystals which would be taken, via a 150 foot shaft sunk into the cliff, to ships waiting in the make-shift harbour at Hole Wyke.

To our right, over the other side of the A174, the mine head buildings of Boulby's modern-day equivalent to this industry loom onto the horizon. The potash mine is Cleveland's only working mine and Britain's only potash pit. Here, ore is extracted from seams 3,774 feet (1,150m) deep, making its shafts the deepest in Europe, and two miles out to sea. It is then refined before being sent by rail to Teesport for shipment and use mainly in agricultural fertilisers. Salt mined in the process may not be as valuable but is of great benefit to local motorists when spread on the roads during wintry weather.

We approach Staithes via the spot from which the most popular postcard shot of the village is always snapped. The centre stage of such pictures is taken up by the famous coble fishing boats (pronounced cobble and distinguishable by their steep bows and flat bottoms) moored in clusters in Staithes Beck.

Squeezed up against the foot of Cowbar Nab, are the cottages of Cowbar and the lifeboat station (unfortunately much-needed both in the winter storms and the summer tourist season) all separated from the larger settlement of Staithes by far more than the inlet. During local government re-organisation in 1974, the powers that be deemed that this narrow stretch of water should represent the county boundary, thus putting the people of Cowbar in Cleveland and their near-neighbours in North Yorkshire. The row over the contrived division has gone on ever since. It's generally agreed that both places should come under the same authority control but no-one seems to be able to decide which one!

We cross over the footbridge — the only low-level link between the two communities — and into Staithes. Once a thriving fishing port to rival Whitby and an early source of ironstone, this charming village now survives as much on tourism as anything else, yet somehow it's managed to retain its original character.

Ocean View, a large, white, double-fronted house on the edge of the shore, has been home to the James family, fish merchants, for 100 years. As we walk towards it, the present occupant, Clem James, is relaxing, feet up, on the balcony. He invites us inside and shows us to two chairs by the picture window so that we can enjoy the incredible panorama out to sea while we chat.

Clem has lived on the seafront here all his life but he's still not regarded as 'local' for his grandfather was a Cornishman! That's how close-knit the Staithes folk are.

"I remember, when I was a kid, this village was insular to the point of isolation. It almost had a language of its own which varied from the next village, not in intonation but in vocabulary," Clem says.

Fishing isn't exactly a thriving industry in Staithes these days but, with two families associated with each of the five full-time boats and associated businesses on shore, it remains the nucleus of the community and, Clem believes, it's what has kept the place from becoming just another "pretty postcard village".

Even so, Clem's seen the face of the village change considerably. It took a long time for electricity, sanitation and water pipes to find their way into homes and, for many years, the community was dominated by a handful of very powerful families. There used to be a fair amount of family rivalry but now, as youngsters move away to find work, there are only fragments left of the Verrill, Theaker and Harrison clans.

"It was nice to be part of a tight-knit community but, on the other hand, Staithes looks smarter and more prosperous now. It was drab and therefore depended on its people to give it life and character — although perhaps that was the era rather than the state of the village," says Clem philosophically.

It's often been said that Staithes folk have Scandinavian origins, for past generations tended to have blond hair and blue eyes. Yet just a few miles down the coast in Runswick Bay, the men were dark and swarthy with flashing teeth, possibly, according to Clem, the products of Spanish sailors whose galleon was shipwrecked nearby.

It is to Runswick Bay that we head next, passing on our climb out of Staithes, Cook's Cottage — part of the Heritage trail and a reminder of Cook's pre-navigation days when he worked for 18 months as an apprentice to a local grocer in a shop long since lost during one of the North Sea's havoc-wreaking tides.

It's an easy three miles to our destination, over fields and around the top of Port Mulgrave where ironstone was once mined and loaded onto ships but where, today, only the short jetty remains, its outer harbour wall having been washed away.

In 1684, the residents of Runswick Bay also experienced this destructive power of the sea when all but one house was washed away in the night. Fortunately,

Rock Cliff, Boulby – the highest on the East coast.

A deserted Port Mulgrave.

It's a dog's life! Left behind by Port Mulgrave fishermen.

the alarm had been raised and no lives were lost.

The village has long since been rebuilt and is now a maze of pretty cottages, crammed together on the cliff side with no roads, only narrow passageways for access. There were working boats moored here as recently as the 1950s but, by 1978, the fishing industry had faded into oblivion. With less than 40 permanent residents, the Bay is now very much a holiday resort with that 'get-away-from-it-all' feeling. The most distinguished visitor has got to be the Marquess of Normanby who had the Thatched Cottage on the point as a Grace and Favour residence. Inland slightly is a tiny Methodist Chapel, built by the women of the village in 1829 and, behind it, one of two springs which provided the village with water until it was connected to the mains supply in the '50s. Another sign of progress is the construction of a car park where once stood herring houses, in which locals stored dried fish.

We seem to have arrived here at the same time as the tide and it's a case of removing shoes and socks and wading, knee-deep, past Hob Holes (caves inhabited by a legendary hob-goblin, renowned for his ability to cure whooping cough) and round to a break in the cliffs. The Way follows a small beck before winding up the hillside to High Cliff where we dry ourselves off. This isn't the first time I am to become closely acquainted with the sea this evening but more of that later...

From here, we follow the line of the cliff edge for over three miles, save for a short diversion inland through Kettleness Farm, until we reach Deep Grove Wyke where a steep descent takes us through a glade of trees (rare so far on the coast), across a stream and down to ground level to follow what was once a railway track serving the three alum quarries that were worked between here and Sandsend.

Erosion of the cliff face has washed away most of the steeping pits in which the alum shale was leached to carry the aluminium salts into solution and has also revealed in the cliff face, part of the tunnel through which the resulting liquor ran to the alum house. This was on the site of the car park which we reach by going down a set of steps and where we end today's journey. The sandstone entrance and exit are formed from the remains of the house.

The tide that was gently creeping ashore at Runswick Bay is now in full flow at Sandsend. Huge waves are battering against the sea wall and, more often than not, crashing over onto the promenade. Simon grins: "A photograph of you looking out to sea would be nice here." Gullible as ever, I agree without considering the consequences ... such as me getting drenched. Oh well, it'll save me taking a shower later!

The road ahead leads eventually into Whitby but, if the tide is out, a walk along the beautiful stretch of sandy beach is to be recommended and will bring you to the foot of the newly-landscaped West Cliff. Two years' work and £3.4 million was invested in an anti-erosion programme which has also involved extending the promenade to try and revitalise this end of Whitby. Owners of properties on the cliff top have been living too close to the edge for comfort and, had the erosion gone on much longer, golfers at the town's club, also up above, may have found themselves teeing off from the crest of a wave, having lost part of the course.

Now though, thanks to a cluster of rocks shipped in from Norway, the value of properties perched on high should reduce no more. Unlike the traditional concrete sea wall, the natural stone armoury breaks up wave energy before it hits the land. They also add character to the area — it's to be hoped a few years' vegetation growth will do the same for the manufactured look of the cliff face.

Chapter Seven

Sixth Section:

WHITBY
TO
BOGGLE HOLE
$7\frac{1}{2}$ miles
TO
SCARBOROUGH
13 miles

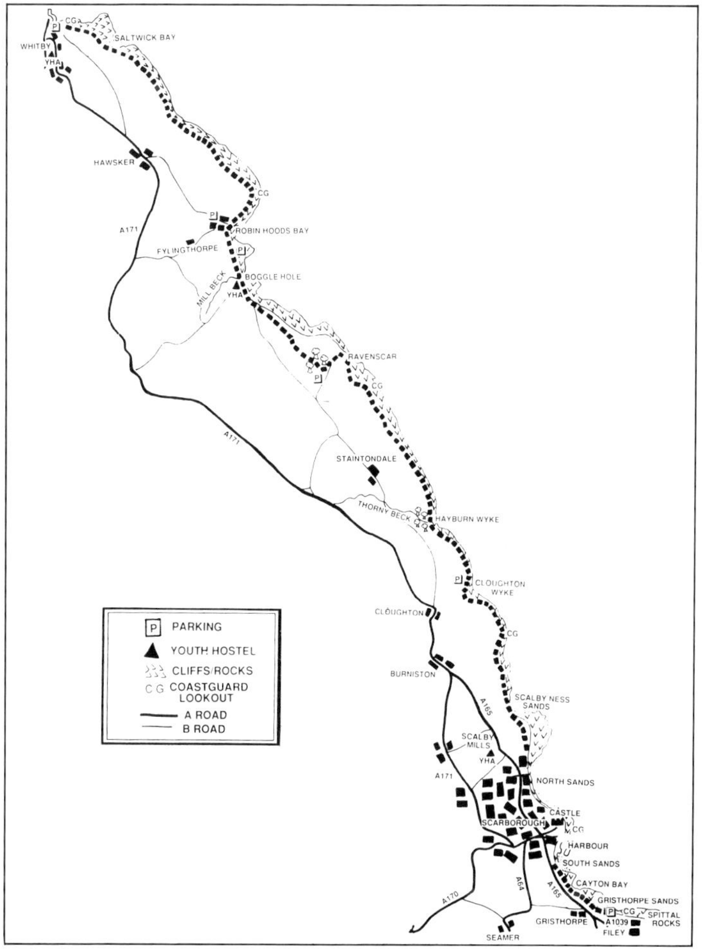

WHEN the sun is high in a blue, cloudless sky, there can be few more splendid sights than Whitby Abbey. When the weather changes, the skies darken and stormy winds swirl around the coastline, it is transformed into a wild but equally dramatic vision that would not be out of place in a Gothic movie.

Silhouetted against the skyline, the old abbey remains the town's most imposing building, even in its ruined state. Whether you are ambling around the local lanes, climbing the headland opposite or sailing in the North Sea, your eye is constantly drawn towards the stunning sandstone mass on top of the East cliff. But its influence over residents and tourists in modern-day Whitby is nothing compared to the role it played in earlier centuries.

There had always been a settlement at this, the safest port between the River Tees and Humber, but it wasn't until the Benedictine monks established themselves on the cliff cap in 1078 that Whitby was put on the map. Travelling traders started passing through and fishing and harbour fees were introduced, collected by monks to begin with until, later in the century, they were re-directed into the town's coffers. And that isn't the only way in which local people benefited.

Because the monastery was a closed one, its occupants built a separate church in which everyone else in the area could worship. St. Mary's parish church, dating back to 1110, is still standing (albeit with a few extensions since then), only yards from the abbey and at the top of the 199 steps that rise up from the town. Still without the benefit of electricity, the use of the church for services is restricted to daylight hours.

But the abbey's authority was not to last. Henry VIII put paid to that and on December 14, 1539, the then Abbot, Henry Davell, surrendered the ecclesiastical buildings to the King's commissioners. The dispersal of the monks created a large gap in the community, led to the closure of the leper hospital and, ultimately, to a changed landscape.

Local historian, Rosalin Barker, is a member of the Friends of Whitby Abbey — a group aiming to draw attention to the whole East cliff area and working towards its conservation and development as a Christian site.

"You can't miss the abbey. Local people are constantly aware of it and are very attached to it but I don't think even they are particularly aware of its history or the relationship between certain bits," she believes.

Recent excavations suggest that the monastery was not the first form of human dwelling but that it was preceded much earlier by a signal station, set up towards the end of Roman rule as a protection against sea raiders. At that time, the place was known as Streonaeshalch meaning the haven of the watch tower.

There are two major events in the Abbey's early history. First, the Synod called by King Oswry in 664 to discuss the Roman and Celtic influence on the timing of Easter celebrations, resulting in the dominance from then on of the former in the north of England. And, secondly, the career of Caedmon, a farmworker-turned-poet, famous for composing the country's first hymn.

The story goes that Caedmon had a vision one night that inspired him to sing about the beginning of creation. When St. Hilda, then in charge at the abbey, heard of this, she encouraged him to enter the monastery where he sang the history of Genesis, the story of Exodus and various other biblical accounts.

A few months after the dissolution, a 21-year-old lease of the abbey site and precinct was granted to Richard Cholmley, a member of the gentry from Kingthorpe near Pickering who later bought the freehold and whose family became one of Whitby's most prevalent. The Cholmleys retained the property until 1791, during which time the house to the south-west of the abbey was rebuilt using, it is thought, stone from the abbey's domestic buildings, hence their non-existence today. Lead was stripped from the church roof and its treasures taken and sold in the south of England but it is the weather that has to take the blame for most of the structural deterioration of Whitby Abbey.

The nave fell in 1762 followed by the south transept a year later and much of the west front before the end of the century. In 1830, it was the turn of the central tower to collapse and the choir suffered damage not long after. Since then, the ruin has altered little, save for some slight effects of German shelling during World War One. Hopefully, conservationists will be able to prevent any future deterioration, while the Friends of Whitby Abbey will be working to preserve its past.

Someone else putting his heart and soul into bringing Whitby's past to life is former engine-driver and hotelier, Rex Greenwood — without doubt one of the town's most prominent personalities. For many years the town-crier, at the age of 65 Rex handed over the role to someone else's younger vocal chords and changed his garb to concentrate instead on Whitby's two most famous characters — Captain James Cook and Count Dracula, both legendary in different senses of the word.

Wearing a period wig and standing erect in a naval costume that cost him over £300 to have made, Rex bears an uncanny resemblance to the sea captain who learned his sailing skills in the town. Not surprisingly, Rex alias James turns more than a few heads as he strides along Whitby's cobbled streets and onto the harbour side from where, telescope to one eye, he surveys the horizon for approaching ships.

"I never smile because Cook never did. He was a very serious person," Rex informs us while, at the same time, insisting that he does not become Cook, but is just himself dressed up. He does though take the responsibility very seriously and has even followed the Cook connection through to Australia where he stole the show at the bicentennial celebrations.

The effect he has as Cook though is nothing to the presence he commandeers when he sweeps through the town's back alleys, hair slicked back, eyes made up to appear bloodshot and two long fangs clearly visible as he curls back his top lip. Dracula is back in town!

Following in the footsteps of the fictional, blood-sucking vampire, Rex takes guided tours around all the places referred to in Bram Stoker's 19th century novel. In it, the Transylvanian Count lands in Whitby at midnight in search of victims. With his fearful expressions, haunting laugh and a touch of dramatic licence, Rex makes sure that the folk he entertains and informs don't forget their visit to Whitby in a hurry. Knowing that, he insists, is the only motivation he needs.

"I'm not an extrovert. I don't do it for myself. I do it because I love people. Just seeing their expressions makes it worth while."

There can't be many grandfathers so tuned into tourism. Rex is one of the best publicity stunts Whitby has, but he does it all off his own back and doesn't make a penny. "Well, what would I be doing otherwise? Probably stuck in some old people's home staring at the television." Somehow, I doubt it! The man's got too much energy and imagination to deprive Whitby's visitors of such colour, fun and warmth.

If you're the type to whom a terrifying night-time tour with Dracula appeals, you may also care to call into Whitby's oldest inhabited building. Bagdale Hall, built in 1516, is now a luxury hotel where, even in closed season, owners Barry and Julie Josey will always be assured of one guest. Unfortunately, Geoffrey the ghost stays uninvited and free of charge!

Legend has it that he's the spirit of Captain Browne Bushell who was executed by Cromwell for treason and has drifted, headless, around the hall ever since in search

The return of Dracula, starring Rex Greenwood.

Deep in the heart of Whitby.

Reflections of Whitby Abbey.

Footsteps in the sand at Saltwick Bay.

of his wife. Mischievous rather than vindictive (hiding the housekeeper's milk money and taking sheets she'd hung to air over the banister rail being two of his more recent tricks), it's rumoured that Geoffrey's presence led to the Old Hall becoming derelict for 15 years until Barry, a former architect and publican, bought it in 1989 for £215,000. "I went for Bagdale because it was Bagdale. Simple as that," says mine host.

But Geoffrey isn't the only squatter in the place. Any unexplained happenings in the kitchen are put down to the ghost of a tramp who once used to hang round there. There's also the strange story of the monkey's plaque in the attic that kept falling to the ground, even after being firmly bolted to a beam. And quite a few visitors to the Hall over the years claim to have seen a white lady floating around the stairwell with her pet dog.

Spooks may be the biggest talking point at Bagdale but it's also an historian's dream, having been owned by a number of principal Whitby people — from the Conyers who had it built, to the Newtons and the Shaw Jeffreys — and still, despite the latest renovations, retaining many ancient features. These include wall panelling and carvings and, outside in the courtyard, a 13th century Venetian well and a 16th century stone sculpture of George and the Dragon, described by Ruskin in his book *Stones of Venice* (from where it originates) as an outstanding work of art.

There's so much to do and see in this lovely harbour town that we could spend a week here and not get bored. We've the final instalment of the Captain Cook Trail to catch up on, for example. This is concluded at the house in Grape Lane where James stayed while working for ship owner John Walker and which is now a museum full of manuscripts, furniture and drawings relating to that period in the would-be sailor's life. On the opposite bank of the River Esk are the shipyards where vessels such as Cook's *Endeavour* and *Discovery* were built.

As we navigate our passage through the crowds to return to our own voyage of discovery on the Cleveland Way, we see plenty of evidence that Whitby has much more to boast about than its links with an 18th century explorer. The Walrus and Carpenter tea rooms remind us that Lewis Carroll composed his poem of that name on the beach here. And the famous Whitby jet is proudly displayed for sale in more than a few shop windows. The black amber is currently undergoing a new lease of life, one hundred years after it lost popularity with the death of Queen Victoria who had immortalised it as a suitable adornment for mourning. During her reign, around 200 Whitby folk were involved in mining jet and over 1500 in making jewellery and ornaments from it. Now, just ten people work with the fossilised wood of the monkey puzzle tree — common in the area 150 million years ago.

And amid all this, the fishing industry continues, bravely battling against EC regulations to maintain Whitby's image of a traditional sea-port. There's still an air of excitement when the boats come in, but it's nothing to the buzz that ran through the community in the days when whales, not cod, were big business. If the waiting wives saw a pair of jaw bones hoisted on the mast, they knew the expedition had been a great success.

Between 1753 and 1833, 55 sailing boats were engaged in whaling from Whitby. It was a dangerous job with the actual killing carried out with barbed harpoons, handheld by crews lowered in small boats down from the larger ship. Thousands of seals and even a few polar bears were slain by this method too, but the best catches were the huge mammals. Great boiler houses on the harbour side turned their blubber into oil, for which there was a high demand throughout the industrial revolution, while the bones were sold for use in corsets. Today, a whalebone arch on West Cliff ensures that the brave whalers of Whitby, many of whom lost their lives in the venture, will never be forgotten. It is also a memorial to Captain William Scoresby, inventor of the crow's nest and, as capturer of 533 whales, the country's champion whaler.

It's the Abbey headland across the estuary though that can claim to be one of the most visited sites in the country. Perhaps it is no coincidence therefore that the

Cleveland Way project officer's survey showed the Whitby section of the walk to be the most well-trodden with more than 112,000 people being logged here in a five-month period of 1989. That's over 100,000 more than at the Hambleton House checkpoint outside Helmsley.

Its popularity is certainly born out on the day we pass through. With holidaymakers wandering to and from their caravan site on the cliff top, it is a good mile before we have the path to ourselves. Before then though, we drop into the coastguard station to check on the weather conditions and tide timings for the next few hours. The sea is calm and the sky is clear, but this time of year is no holiday for Marine Rescue workers.

Busy though they are, they'd rather people telephoned or called in for advice than got themselves into difficulty later. But with the boom in leisure pursuits, small boat accidents are increasingly commonplace and it's the coastguards who co-ordinate maritime search and rescue operations all around the British coastline and for up to 1,000 miles into the North Atlantic. In an emergency, they call on the RNLI, the Royal Navy and the RAF as well as merchant shipping, commercial aircraft and ferries.

They don't just deal with incidents at sea though —cliff tops come under their jurisdiction too. In charge of the coastline from Port Mulgrave to Hayburn Wyke is Craig Allison, who oversees 11 auxiliary guards based at each of the four stations in his section — Whitby, Kettleness, Robin Hood's Bay and Ravenscar. The sea should be respected, says Craig, even by people who have no intention of coming into close contact with it. Fossil hunters or sunbathers, for example, should always be alert: they've been known to become so absorbed in their pastime that they find themselves cut off by the tide, Craig warns. And sailors should always carry flares and life-jackets and make sure someone on dry land knows they are out at sea. "Take every precaution before you set out," he advises.

Such sensible advice and so easy to follow. Why, we wonder, do some people still choose to ignore it year after year? Confident that *we* should be OK as long as we keep to the path, we stride out once more. Ahead of us are the final laps of the Cleveland Way and they can be quite time-consuming. With good planning over a few days though, they can be just as rewarding in their own way as some of the harder climbs or the scenery of the more remote sections.

Looking down on the smooth sands of Saltwick Bay — the only real beach between here and Robin Hood's Bay — it's understandable why campers congregating above eventually led to the creation of a holiday village here. Its residents, of whom there are thousands in peak season, seem today to be drawn to Whitby like bees to a honey pot while, for us going in the opposite direction, civilisation soon becomes an unknown quantity.

It seems strange that a route which wends its way around such magnificent coastline isn't teeming with ramblers. It can't be that it's just our lucky day for there's plenty of evidence of under-usage in the amount of undergrowth covering the track and the number of knee-high nettles we need to avoid, particularly as there isn't a dock leaf in sight. In fact, we meet no-one until we come in sight of Robin Hood's Bay — the beach that is, not the village for that is hidden from us all the time we are rounding Ness Point (otherwise known as North Cheek) to enter it at the top end. Incidentally, the land formation at the far side of the gulf is, not surprisingly, known as South Cheek, or Old Peak.

If you're unlucky enough to arrive here in the midst of swirling sea fret, you can do nothing save consider it an experience! The mist can blanket Bay (as it's abbreviated locally) when the next village up the valley is bathed in warm sunlight. It creates a chilling and eerie atmosphere which brings visitors to a halt while residents carry on regardless.

My only previous visit to Bay was during a sixth-form field trip and my abiding memory is of the geography teacher enthusing over the "wonderful" wave-cut platforms. This time, the rock beds are hidden by the sea

Night-time amusements at Scarborough.

Just one cornet – oh!

Millions of pounds of fish are landed each year in Scarborough harbour.

and I can concentrate instead on the incredible network of alleys, steep slopes and steps that give the village its identity, but around which we were not allowed to wander during that first brief encounter when we were marched down the hill to sketch and then marched back to the top again.

If you are fascinated by geology, do plan your arrival to coincide with low tide so that you can study with dry feet the faultline running seaward, the scars of hard rock, the erratic boulders transported from the Lake District during the ice age of 10,000 years ago, and the sandstones that haven't strayed very far from their original site at Ravenscar but have travelled all the same.

The majority of sightseers to Bay though are attracted by the charm of a place that has changed little for decades, despite the loss of fishing as its major money earner, and by the excitement of its famous (or should that be infamous?) smuggling past.

At its peak, the village was more important to the fishing industry than Whitby was and the whole community was involved in ensuring its continued success. While the men were out at sea in their cobles and herring boats, the women baited lines and barrelled fish for market, while young boys mended nets and made lobster pots. Then, like many other places through which we've travelled on the Cleveland Way, the railway arrived and influenced life here more than anyone could have imagined. It not only widened the market for fish but it encouraged visitors, some of whom liked the place so much they built houses around the station at the top of the bank and moved in.

Down in The Dock, life went on much as before but the increase in business brought about by improved transportation proved to be the lull before the storm. As boat sizes increased, the tiny port without any harbour facilities was unable to cope and the industry waned to such an extent that by the 1920s only two families were still fishing. It's been revitalised of late but tourism is now the main source of income for the locals — the genuine ones of whom are hard to find among the incomers who

A leafy trail to Robin Hood's Bay.

have either retired here or who only spend part of the year in their little Yorkshire hideaway holiday home.

Fishing isn't the only thing that has done a disappearing act over the years. During a two-century period, the ferocity of the North Sea caused 200 houses to slip into the water, heavily depleting the amount of accommodation in the original nucleus settlement of Baytown. A sea wall built in 1975 should hopefully prevent a repeat performance! Some of the oldest houses, dating back to the early 1600s can be found on King Street while the smallest are in the Fisherhead district where the fishermen lived so they could keep an eye on the grassy shore where they kept their cobles.

Connecting cellars and cupboards between many of the buildings in Bay made policing it a nightmare for excisemen. It is claimed that a bale of silk could be passed from the bottom of the village to the top without ever seeing daylight, while another complicated network of passageways linked the public houses and came out at King's Beck.

There are two museums in Robin Hood's Bay. One is tiny and traditional; the other, in a converted warehouse, more of an indoor theme park. Here a series of scenes, created by former toy-maker and rock-climbing tutor, Richard Leak, take the visitor back in time to the mid-18th century when smuggling was a way of life for some. With recreated street, pub and ship scenes, many with sound effects, the illegal operations are made to seem exciting but are not glorified — the screams of a convicted wool smuggler having his right hand cut off are enough to make anyone glad those days have long since gone.

The Smuggling Experience, which you'll come across before reaching the bank top car park, has proved a great hit especially with school parties and entertained more than 200,000 visitors in 1988, its first year. It's open from 10 am-6 pm, Spring to October.

The Cleveland Way leaves Bay via a right-hand turning just before The Dock and, although Ravenscar seems to be only around the corner, we soon realise how much truth there really is in the saying 'appearances can be deceptive' for we have to add a good three miles to our total to date before finally making it to the next headland.

If you've dallied in Whitby and Robin Hood's Bay, and you find yourself running out of daylight hours, the youth hostel at Boggle Hole could be a convenient overnight stop with Ravenscar your post-breakfast goal. Nestled among trees in a secluded inlet (reachable along the beach from Bay if the tide is out), the hostel hogs an exclusive view out to sea. If it weren't for the fact that our car's in Scarborough, I think we'd be tempted to find an excuse to stay. We won't find many other places too ideally placed for a refreshing early morning paddle!

Just short of Ravenscar, we are forced by a ravine to turn inland slightly and past the shale waste tips of yet more alum works. What makes this more worthy of note than the rest is that it's the only site where the alum house has survived. Which is why the National Trust is confident that the former industrial complex — thought to be the country's most comprehensive surviving monument to the manufacture of alum — has the potential to become a tourist attraction. Despite decades of neglect since the mine ceased production in 1860, parts of old warehouses and joiners' and blacksmiths' workshops can still be identified.

Archaeologist Garry Marshall was employed in 1990 to spend three years uncovering more details and supervising conservation work with the eventual aim of admitting members of the public onto the site to give them an insight into the East Coast's industrial heritage.

"The alum house won't be rebuilt because, to be quite honest, we don't know what they looked like as a whole because they closed down before the era of photography. But as you look down on this one, you can see the layout of the rooms and, from documentation, we have a good idea of what the contents of each would have been," Garry explained.

The National Trust owns a mile of the coastal cliff here and has an information centre alongside the Cleveland Way, just before the path reaches the road into the

Scarborough's South Bay from Wheatcroft Cliff.

The last rays of sunlight cast a rosy glow over Scarborough.

Filey – an illuminating resort in which to end the trek.

Take your pick.

village. Turning left onto it, we face seaward to where a Roman signal station once stood but where now, blocking our view of where sea meets sky, is the hiker-friendly Ravenhall Hotel. It has little choice but to welcome walkers because as well as being on our route, it's the finishing point for the Lyke Wake Walk. No doubt the hotel staff have revived many a weary wanderer who arrives a shadow of the figure that set off with such gusto at least 16 hours previous. Little wonder that a coffin-shaped badge is the reward for those who make it! 'Give me the Cleveland Way any day', I muse as I stride jauntily down Station Road.

Ravenscar isn't exactly a thriving little community but it might have been had the dreams of turn-of-the-century planners come true. They saw the high cliff top with its magnifient views as a tourist venue to rival Whitby and Scarborough and, having bought the land, they set to —designing road routes, installing sewers and even selling a few plots. But in 1913, the development company went bankrupt and no-one saw fit to pursue its cause. The closure of the railway station in the 1960s only added to the village's isolation and the sense of desolation is magnified by thoughts of 'what might have been'. Still, we find plenty of consolation in the fact that walking along the edge of farm fields is much more pleasant than trying to dodge amusement arcades and ice-cream stalls, which are what might have eventually developed from the seeds sown by those Victorian gentlemen.

It was blowing a gale while we were slightly inland at Ravenscar, but here on the cliff edge we are sheltered by the pastures of waist-high corn on one side and, to the other, by shrubs and trees that have so far survived shore-bound landslips, but which are barely recognisable, having been re-shaped by the full force of cold North Sea winds.

When I say we are on the cliff edge, I'm not exaggerating. Not being too keen on heights, I'm very tempted to close my eyes, so terrifyingly steep is the drop. But, as Simon wisely points out, walking blind is not a good idea under the circumstances — one wrong move and I could be taking an early bath!

Much of the Cleveland Way from here to the end takes us through similar scenery — all very pleasant and, today, quite a suntrap. However, one can only enthuse about clear blue sea, crashing waves and rock formations for so long. Hayburn Wyke therefore comes as a delightful and welcome surprise. The deserted, if somewhat rocky, cove is tempting enough but it's the sylvan slopes of the creek and the bubbling waterfall cascading onto the shore that make this nature reserve well-worth revisiting when an afternoon of fresh air and solitude is required.

The 65-acres surrounding the convergence point of two streams was donated to the National Trust in 1981 and is managed by them jointly with the Yorkshire Wildlife Trust. It's a rich habitat for birds with the conifers providing excellent nesting sites and the sea bringing in gannets, cormorants, kittiwakes and oystercatchers. Under the trees grow lush ferns, mosses, rushes and woodland flowers such as primrose and foxglove. Little wonder that the Victorians used to come here on excursions from York and Scarborough and have tea at the nearby hotel (still here).

The descent to Hayburn Beck was made easy thanks to steps created by local scouts many years ago but, as I have discovered many times over the last few weeks of walking the Way, what goes down inevitably goes up again and we face a steep climb to get back to the top of the cliff at Tindall Point on the other side. There are obviously many visitors to this spot as jaded (make that 'unfit') as I for the seat halfway up looks well-used. The unhindered view back along the coast which it affords provides a good excuse for a sit down if you don't want to admit your fatigue but I don't think I'll get away with that. Simon, on the other hand, doesn't need to justify his pauses. He's been carring 1½ stone of camera gear over his shoulder all this way so I suppose he's entitled to the occasional break!

As we make our way round to the next Wyke (the

After 108 miles, we're not going to let a little rain spoil our celebrations!

Archaeologist Garry Marshall uncovers Ravenscar's industrial history.

name given to small inlets along the Yorkshire coast), Scarborough Castle is clearly visible on the horizon. We never seem to get any closer though and, if you've any sense, you'll arrange to have a support party waiting at Cloughton Wyke — there's a road right here from Cloughton — and hitch a lift the rest of the way to the resort. You'll have hiked a fair distance if you've come from Whitby in one session and won't miss anything except more sea views between here and Scalby Mills where the path comes to a temporary halt close to a new sea life centre and not far from the town's youth hostel.

Gluttons for punishment that we are, we walk on, arriving hot, tired and thirsty at the north end of Scarborough. The castle, perched on the limestone cragg is still out of reach but — and here we have a confession to make — now only a short bus ride away!

Bright and blooming Robin Hood's Bay, while dark clouds threaten Ravenscar ahead.

Beautiful and refreshing Hayburn Wyke.

Chapter Eight

Seventh Section:

SCARBOROUGH TO FILEY 11.2 miles

THE NORTH Bay is the quieter of Scarborough's two, and more pleasant to walk along, although all this may change once a proposed multi-million-pound holiday village and entertainment complex is developed. If you have the energy to make your way into the town by foot, there's a promenade going right around the headland or you can go up to the top and drop down to the other side behind or via the castle. If not, both open-topped and enclosed double deckers run every few minutes from the Corner Café, along Marine Drive and onto the Foreshore.

If you take a look at the map, you'll see that the Cleveland Way takes a leap and bypasses the town altogether which, in the summer, is not a bad idea. Unless, that is, you or your children found Whitby too quaint. In that case, South Bay with its fun parks, slot machines, fortune-tellers and joke shops will be more up your street and make it well-worth your making Scarborough your base while walking the coastal stretch of the Cleveland Way.

For thousands of kids — and many adults too — the seaside and ice-cream go together as naturally as sand and shells. In Scarborough, Jaconelli and ice-creams are equally synonomous. And the man behind them, Peter, is as hard to miss as his numerous cafés along the south prom.

He's as wide as he is tall, has a wonderful self-deprecating sense of humour and gold-capped teeth that glint whenever he roars with laughter, which is often. He also holds the title of World Oyster Eating Champion 1971! And on top of running a successful business, he spent 30 years as a borough councillor, retiring in May 1991, and is a former Mayor. In short, Peter Jaconelli is the nearest you'll get to a Mr. Scarborough. Which is amazing considering he's a Glaswegian of Italian descent!

His father bought the first shop on Foreshore Road in 1947 on the site purported to be the very spot where explorers landed when they discovered Scarborough. "No-one's old enough to dispute it so that's what I tell everybody," Peter chuckles.

He took over the business when he left the army. Since then, the style and character of the shop have remained the same, but the list of available flavours has extended somewhat beyond the original vanilla, chocolate and lemon. Jaconelli ice-cream is now sold all over and, in 1989, was voted best in the country by the national ice-cream alliance. Peter's now keen to travel and find good-taste fans further afield — he reckons he can teach the American manufacturers a thing or two! — but Scarborough, he insists, will always be his home. "It's so natural," he explains. "Wherever you stand, you can see the cliffs."

It's incredible really to think that the things which appeal to 20th century society — the cliffs and the sea — are the very same that persuaded the Romans to settle here and build a signal station in 370 AD to warn of impending raids. The remains of the station were revealed by archaeologists in the 1920s. They also unearthed evidence of inhabitation as early as the Iron Age, again on Castle Hill. Since the 12th century though when the Earl of Albemarle built the first, the headland has always hosted a fort. And amazingly, despite five sieges over the centuries plus bombing by the Germans in the First World War, there's still a substantial ruin to be explored. If you climb onto the battlements, you'll see the identical aspect of surrounding land and sea that will have faced King John and Edward during their reputed visits to the Castle.

Scarborough's status as a Royal Garrison town declined after the Civil War when, despite a determined stand, the Castle eventually surrendered to Parliament. But almost at the same time, an important discovery was made that gave Scarborough a different reputation and one that it's kept to this very day — that of a holiday resort.

Today's tourism chiefs owe everything to a Mrs. Elizabeth Farrar, wife of a local gentleman, who, in 1620, discovered natural springs bubbling out beneath South Cliff (just about where the Spa ballroom stands now). Ignorant of its high sulphate content, all Mrs. Farrar knew was that the water tasted bitter and stained the rock. But that was enough to persuade her that it had medicinal qualities and, on that whim alone, Scarborough developed as a fashionable Spa town. By the time people stopped taking the waters in the mid-19th century, its popularity was so well-established that crowds continued to flock here for entertainment and relaxation.

"Scarborough was a very go-ahead place in the 1700s and 1800s," declares Marie Belfitt, teacher of Local History at the technical college who, through research on the subject discovered, among other things, that bathers were expected to dip in the nude and drink five pints of water a day in order to reap its benefits.

"It could apparently cure anything from constipation to madness and infertility, but I imagine the holiday itself had as much a part to play in making visitors feel better," she laughs. "Even so, Scarborough would not be the place it is today if it wasn't for Mrs. Farrar's beliefs."

With great pride and insatiable enthusiasm, Marie rattles through Scarborough's other boasts, such as its beach chalets being the first in England and it having the first-ever open-air pool to be filled by the tide. The literary Sitwell family lived here in their early days, she continues, and their home at Wood End is now a

Master Mariner and part-time marmalade maker, Captain Sydney Smith

museum. And Anne Brontë died here while staying at The Grand. (I bet that didn't do a lot for the hotel's reputation!).

Then of course, there was the famous Scarborough Fayre — the longest and best-known of England's medieval fairs, having been granted a charter in 1253 and lasting for 45 days between August and September each year. Merchants came from all over England, Europe and Scandinavia and the whole town was transformed into one large market place with goods often being exchanged by bartering. The last fayre is thought to have been held in 1788, but it has never been officially abolished by Parliament. Its modern-day equivalent is a fortnight of art and entertainment events in June.

"And don't forget about the fishing," Marie adds. "Scarborough was the fifth largest herring port and, in its heyday, attracted train loads of people coming to watch the barrelling. The women had to bandage their fingers with strips of flour cloth to stop them getting gangrene because the knives were so sharp and the salt they used caused infections... but if you want to know about fishing, you'd best go and see old Captain Smith."

So we do, arriving just as the Master Mariner has finished making marmalade. And this, as we soon discover, is only one of many pursuits which prove that, at the age of 83, Captain Sydney Thomas Smith is not the type to relax in retirement.

He's the editor of the *Fisherman's Nautical Almanac* — an annual 700-page directory of the country's fishing vessels, still drives a car (although he's thinking of selling it because he can never find anywhere to park in Scarborough) and, most incredibly, is a member of a rowing club! "I was in a crew twice last summer. Rowing's no trouble to me. I was brought up on it. I never remember learning but I know I could row before I could walk," says Syd modestly.

Those were the days, he points out, when the sea was clean because sewage pipes didn't discharge into it. He believes it was pollution that killed off the herrings and took away a very important source of income for local families. From May to October, he remembers, the men would catch herring while the women found seasonal work preparing the fish on the quayside:

"It was a very skilled job and very quick they were with the barrels. As the boats landed the herring, it was bought straight away. The buyer would bring the fish in baskets to where the women were seated around barrels — a full-time cooper was employed too — and tip them into the troughs. The women used to gyp (gut) them and pack them in salt — a layer of salt and a layer of herrings with the heads all t' centre 'til the barrel was filled up and the cooper filled it with brine."

"Trains used to run trips. I don't know what time they left West Riding but they used to arrive in Scarborough about six in' mornin'. When they got to the station, there was a crowd of café touts waiting for them: "Come and 'ave breakfast down 'ere'. Bertie Whitaker used to 'ave a restaurant on' foreshore and he made a fortune out of it —'Shilling Dinners' — anything you liked as long as it was sausage and mash. He finished up owning half the foreshore!"

Far from putting him off fish for life, Capt. Smith still can't get enough of it, although he admits it doesn't taste quite the same as when it's caught fresh from the sea with your own fair hands. "My father used to say to me: 'Go down and get boat oot and get 'alf a bucket of herring and fetch 'em home if you want any breakfast'. I used to be down on pier about half five on the morning. We used to have fried herrings for breakfast straight from the sea, then we had 'em rolled at tea-time, baked in vinegar."

On other occasions, Syd's mother would send him to see his Aunt Liza in the Kipper House and ask for a 'pennorth' of broken kippers. These were ones that had been torn as they were removed from the nails on which they hung over oak smoke fires.

Today's fishermen working from Scarborough harbour concentrate on white fish, mostly cod and haddock, and in 1989-90 landed catch worth over £3½ million. Merchant ships during the same period handled over 30,000 tonnes of cargo — timber, fertilizer, barley,

Lick father, lick son!

Headroom is limited through this archway of blackthorn bushes.

potatoes and wheat. Since Captain Smith worked in the harbour-master's office in the early '70s, the number of cargo vessels being controlled from there has almost halved. For the last ten years, the old man has been campaigning for the introduction of more strenuous anti-pollution measures, for he predicts that unless the sea is cleaned up, the decline will continue and eventually fishing will disappear altogether, leaving Scarborough purely a tourist spot. It always attracted visitors, the widower agrees, but the advent of the motorcar and the amusement arcades have changed the face of the town to one he doesn't particularly like.

"When I were a lad, all them buildings on' sand side that are now shops and places with machines that you put your money into, they were all fishermen's houses and ship's chandlers and stores. There used to be a big rock manufacturer on The Foreshore and you could see rock being made. Old Rocky who kept it used to sell us broken rock — to local lads it was a ha'penny a bag: to visiting lads, it was a penny. Our cheeks used to stick out with pieces ... it would last all day," Syd muses. "People living in Scarborough now aren't local and the sea is something new to them. They don't realise the power of it. Its power is infinite."

For this lively pensioner with his tattooed forearms, the sea holds no fear and he still sails out of the harbour every November to lay a wreath on the waves in memory of those who have lost their lives at sea — formerly as shipowners and latterly as fishermen. Captain Smith, the last of the long line with no children to continue it, is the only one to have trained as an officer in the merchant navy and spend many years away from his home town: the town where his love of the sea began when, as an infant, he joined his father on fishing trips and where he saw out his working days as deputy harbour-master.

We haven't even got onto his personal recollections of life on the world's ocean waves when it is time to bid farewell to Captain Smith. We leave clutching a jar of marmalade. Fortunately, we only have two or three hours' walk ahead of us before we can sample the parting gift from our new-found friend.

Once beyond the Spa complex, where, incidentally Max Jaffa entertained audiences for 26 years, we leave the crowds behind and begin winding our way up the landscaped bank to the esplanade, under the clock tower and towards the car park. Looking back, we get our best view yet of the sweeping bay between us and the dominant castle.

Gales from the sea have bent a line of blackthorn bushes into a delightful archway and we are drawn into the natural tunnel, anxious to see what awaits us at the other side. All the guide books we have read have a habit of dismissing the next, and final, nine miles as an anti-climax but we are far from disappointed. Three bays lie between here and Filey Brigg which in turn create a number of headlands, each with its own identity, for us to master.

South Cliff Golf Course is almost as close to the edge of Wheatcroft Cliff as the fairways were at Whitby, but we are left a little space in which to walk and their luscious greens make a nice change from some of the parched fields that we skirted on our approach to Scarborough. To the north of Cornelian Bay — named after the reddish-yellow gemstones found there in the past — is White Nab and the worryingly (and no doubt appropriately) labelled Perilous Rocks at its foot.

Here, the path drops down into a ravine and up through trees — the first of many in the short stretch before Cayton Bay. The woods at Knipe/Osgodby Point (nearby Osgodby village was mentioned in the Domesday Book) are owned by the National Trust and again the path becomes something of a switchback until it levels out above Cayton Sands — a super stretch of beach that, not surprisingly, led to the formation of a holiday camp only yards away across the main A165 road and which, more recently, has proved a great attraction to surfers.

A strong, biting, westerly wind makes for slow progress but the cloudless sapphire sky serves to

Edging ever closer to our final destination, one bay at a time.

Only a few yards left to the tip of Filey Brigg.

emphasise the beauty of this coastline and we find ourselves gasping at the view almost every time we round a corner. The peace is broken though as we approach Lebberston Cliff where nesting gulls make it quite clear that they don't like being disturbed. They refuse to settle or shut up until we are well out of the way.

As we go, we see the clearest evidence yet of the effects of erosion. Great lumps of land and, a little further, slabs of concrete Second World War pillboxes can be seen two hundred feet below, laid to rest as it were after a momentous landslide. Cracks growing steadily into large gaps have already begun to appear at the side of our path, signalling which chunks of the cliff will be next to fall. Little wonder that notices warning us away from the edge are positioned every few yards.

A caravan site and holiday park above Gristhorpe Sands are the only blots on the landscape today but we train our eyes instead on the view we have been longing for all these 100-odd miles — Carr Naze, the Filey promontory that marks our final frontier. The official finishing line comes some way before then, on the North/East Riding border but there's no indication of its exact point (unless you're counting stiles, in which case it's the second of two coming up to the final big bend!). And as it's in the middle of nowhere on Newbiggin cliff, don't expect many guests to turn up to your celebration party!

Part of the long-term strategy of the Cleveland Way Project Manager is to make Filey Brigg the recognised end before 1993. There's also talk among Filey councillors of placing a register in the Tourist Information Office where walkers can record their achievement. At least then we, and everyone else, would have proof that we made it.

As it is, we opt anyway for completion at the tip of the Brigg. Once there, we are further east than we've ever been on the Cleveland Way — and where better to scream and jump for joy at our mammoth pedestrian feat?

Filey, a miniature Scarborough without the tackiness, is a choice place to unwind. A community that developed around the fresh water ravine and fishing went on, with the arrival of the railway, to attract Victorian gentry on vacation. To its credit, Filey has retained many of the old-fashioned values of those days, making it a favourite resort of the young and old alike. Its six miles of safe sands, sheltered by the gritstone Brigg at one end and the chalky white cliffs of Flamborough Head at the other, are great for children. Their grandparents, on the other hand, generally prefer to stroll around the colourful Crescent Gardens that helped the town win the regional Britain in Bloom award three years running at the end of the eighties.

The whole of The Crescent — its row of white, four and five-storey houses, all with a sea view and fronting onto the beautiful flower beds — was paid for and designed by a Birmingham solicitor in the mid-1830s and, says twice town-mayor Michael Fearon, still plays a central role in creating Filey's unique identity.

"Mr. Unett was a man of vision and we are very grateful that he ploughed his profits into developing The Crescent area with some degree of foresight," comments Mr. Fearon, a Filey man born and bred and something of an expert on its history. "He gave us gardens that are the glory of Filey in the summer."

Fishing is still important to the community — the Coble Landing being a hive of activity and also the site of the town's newly-built lifeboat station and boat. But tourism is now its mainstay.

Audrey Goodall and her late husband Harry holidayed in Filey for more than 30 years before deciding to move up here from their home near Sheffield and open a guest-house. With her experience, first as a visitor and then as a resident of ten years plus, there aren't many better placed than Audrey to explain what it is about Filey that makes people return time after time:

"It's so peaceful and the people here are so wonderful, so very, very friendly. There's no commercialism and it's an ideal centre for the Wolds and the North York Moors," she enthuses. "As a place to live and a place to visit, it's wonderful. It gets busy in the summer but nothing like the large seaside towns. You know what they say — 'Small is Beautiful'. And you couldn't find a better example of that than Filey."

Apart from the beach, the bay and the Brigg, Filey's other commendable aspects include its country park on the top of Wool Dale cliffs, often frequented by ornithologists; its Edwardian festival — a week of traditional family entertainment at the beginning of July; and it's the footpath kingdom of the North. It's the start or finish (however you care to look at it) of the Wolds Way, stretching to North Ferriby near Hull, the newly-recognised Centenary Way (80 miles from York) and, as if we could forget, the by now very familiar Cleveland Way.

Which reminds us. Ever since we took our first steps on the Cleveland Way many weeks ago, we have been promising ourselves a paddle in the sea on arrival at Filey. Well, it may be seven o'clock in the evening and it may be raining but here goes ...

BIBLIOGRAPHY/RECOMMENDED READING

* *Cleveland Way* — National Trust Guide by Ian Sampson: Published in 1989 by the Countryside Commission and ideal as a step-by-step navigational guide.

* *The Cleveland Way — Yorkshire Moors and Coast Footpath* by Bill Cowley. First published in 1967, since when some of the route has changed slightly but it's still good for background details, local history and geography.

* *The Cleveland Way* by Alan Falconer. This book preceded Ian Sampson's as the Countryside Commission's guide. Details of the route itself are very sketchy and even the reproduced Ordnance Survey maps are out of date, but Falconer's chapters on the geology, natural world, industry and development in general of his beloved Cleveland are full of facts.

* *The North York Moors — Landscape Heritage*, edited by D. A. Spratt and B. J. D. Harrison.

* *The History of Saltburn* by Chris Scott Wilson.

* Thanks to the *Evening Gazette* newspaper for permission to reproduce some of the photographs used in the series that inspired our book.

* A special thank you to all the people who gave up their time to talk to us along the way and share their knowledge and memories.